CAPITALISM: UNJUST, UNSTABLE, & UNSUSTAINABLE

HENRY GEORGE AND JEAN BAPTISTE SAY REVISITED

BENJAMIN BATTERSBY

iUniverse, Inc.
New York   Bloomington

iUniverse books may be ordered through booksellers or by contacting:

iUniverse
1663 Liberty Drive
Bloomington, IN 47403
www.iuniverse.com
1-800-Authors (1-800-288-4677)

Because of the dynamic nature of the Internet, any Web addresses or links contained in this book may have changed since publication and may no longer be valid. The views expressed in this work are solely those of the author and do not necessarily reflect the views of the publisher, and the publisher hereby disclaims any responsibility for them.

ISBN: 978-1-4401-8793-3 (sc)
ISBN: 978-1-4401-8795-7 (ebook)
ISBN: 978-1-4401-8794-0 (hc)

Printed in the United States of America

iUniverse rev. date: 12/23/2009

INTRODUCTION

It will almost certainly be considered strange, bizarre, and quixotic, if not ludicrous, that virtually a century and a quarter after the appearance of Henry George's, *Progress and Poverty* someone not a professional economist should undertake an inquiry of the subject matter of his great work with a view not only to validating George's findings, but to amending them in certain cases from the perspective of the new twenty-first century's global. neo-capitalistic era.

This inquiry will revive the terms "political economy" and "political economist" to replace the terms "economy" and "economist," not only to comport with George's terminology, but also to properly reconnect the truncated appellation to its inherent political dimension.

It is surely appropriate that someone not formally trained in political economy, like George himself, and therefore not vested in any particular school of economics, should undertake a review and revitalization of such a neglected work of genius as George's.

While hordes of economists have been produced by institutions of higher learning over the past six decades or so, almost all are employed in either government, corporate entities, or academia, where the conventional wisdom absorbed from their conventional predecessors is utilized to probe the statistical entrails provided to them by their mentors. They are generally engaged in estimating the growth prospects of an industry from quarter to quarter (frequently disguising unpleasant prospects), but almost never raising the issue of persistent and seemingly ineradicable poverty within the enormously rich modern societies, and certainly not the prognosis for Capitalism's survival into the future in its present form.

Consequently, this work is not directed at the compromised specialist in government, corporation, or academia, but at the thoughtful questioning citizen of ordinary powers of reasoning, sufficiently educated at the "University of Life."

This inquiry will generally follow the path first laid out by George in the belief that his groundwork is essential to the task of following his extraordinary insights and reasoned constructs, not only through the era in which he lived, but with modified application to and through the Capitalistic explosion in the era of the "Robber Barons." The insights of Jean Baptiste Say, in describing the intimate and unbreakable link between production and consumption, are then tapped into in proceeding into the present, where corporate possession of world-wide natural and physical endowments—particularly all manner of energy sources—shows evidence of trumping the vast industrial complexes of previously dominating national economies.

Those who have not read *PROGRESS AND POVERTY* are encouraged to do so, not only as an aid to understanding this present, expanded inquiry, but also to make the acquaintance of this passionately moral man with a heart as large as his intellect and courage.

Those who have never heard of either *PROGRESS AND POVERTY*, or its author Henry George, may well place blame for this deprivation at the feet of those who, incapable of refuting his powerful vision, and wholly in the paid service of the beneficiaries of falsehood and self-serving error, have successfully entombed the genius of Henry George by mocking him as "the single tax" advocate, and otherwise ignoring him and the towering intellectual edifice he constructed in 1879.

The author will frequently refer the reader to the original source for .greater detail and explication than the thrust of his argument, in his view, requires or justifies.

Hopefully, the reader will understand that the author of this work, in quoting and encapsulating *PROGRESS AND POVERTY,* does not vouch for each and every statement or the eternal relevance of same. Aspects of our current service economy, for example, could hardly have been clearly anticipated. So let us begin this expanding journey into our own fateful era of global Capitalism.

FORWARD

Henry George's introduction to *PROGRESS AND POVERTY*, appropriately entitled "The Introductory Problem," enunciated the inquiry to be pursued in his book, namely the basis for the continuing, and ever-increasing, poverty among the working class concurrent with the increasing wealth of the community as a whole. Intuitively, one would have supposed that the working class would, at least, have maintained from stage to stage of growing community wealth, a similar proportionate share. That this did not occur, and that the greater the wealth of cities such as London, New York, Paris, etc., the deeper the poverty of the unemployed and unemployable poor, was apparent to George, as well as to others, in the latter part of the nineteenth century, when wealth, visible and tangible, bedecked the great cities.

It was apparent to George that periodic "hard times" were certainly connected with material progress, and represented paroxysms occurring in the course of such growth. Such paroxysms were most likely to occur where population was most dense, the machinery of production and exchange most highly developed, and all the benefits and efficiencies of a highly developed infrastructure existed to provide the social efficiencies of public transportation, water supply, sewage disposal, lighted streets, etc. It was certainly a paradox, and drew the attention of thoughtful persons, sages, and those eagerly engaged in deflecting criticism from the rich and powerful, the greatest beneficiaries of swelling overall wealth.

Not only was George impelled to seek the answer to the paradox he observed all about him due to compassion for the "have nots," but because he understood that such inequities could only, in the future, spell upheaval and disaster, as had happened virtually without fail throughout history. Perhaps to find the answer would lead to a cure.

In a subsequent chapter of his book, Henry George almost inadvertently amended the preceding vision of labor receiving an ever-decreasing share of community wealth production by postulating that, while labor's *percentile* share of all produced wealth must certainly diminish through the depredations of ever-increasing rent (the return to land—one of the three factors of production), in an advanced community blessed with a high, mutually supportive population, swiftly expanding technology and education, benign and reasonably honest and efficient governance, the *absolute* return to labor of its share of swelling community-produced wealth, might indeed keep pace with or even exceed previously experienced historical levels.

In this particular vision, we may have a partial explanation of the increasing standard of living of the citizens of Western Europe and the United States through the twentieth century, particularly following the Great Depression and active government intervention to ensure the expansion of national economies. It must be stressed that, whereas George spoke of land as one of the three factors in the distribution of produced wealth, the other two being labor and capital, he wrote of land, not only as the surface of the earth employed for agricultural production, but as "all natural endowments." For purposes of clarification, at an appropriate point in the expounding of this narrative, the term "natural resources" will be employed in lieu of "land."

The term "land" was initially used by early political economists because the agricultural model of labor and capital applied to farming estates was the only one recognizable.

TABLE OF CONTENTS

1

THE WAGES FUND

The conventional economic wisdom of Henry George's time, having drawn upon the insights and published studies of prior generations of political economists, essentially philosophers and clergymen of comfortable means dependent upon the great landowners of Britain, was that of the "wages fund." This theory stressed that the amount of money available for the wages of the laboring population was wholly dependent upon the totality of capital available for the payment of wages. If capital was abundant, then higher wages could be paid out or more laborers could be employed, unless and until the population expanded and wages would necessarily fall due to being more widely spread.

This particular doctrine held almost total sway, not only among the upper classes and academicians, but among such elements of the working class as were inclined to ponder the issue.

George observed that this theory simply did not correspond to the obvious facts. If wages depended upon the ratio between the amount of labor seeking employment and the amount of capital devoted to its employment, the relative scarcity or abundance of one factor must mean the relative abundance or scarcity of the other. Therefore capital must be relatively abundant where wages are high and relatively scarce where wages are low. Now, as the capital used in paying wages must largely consist of the capital constantly seeking investment, the current rate of interest must be the measure of its relative abundance or scarcity. So, if it is true that wages depend upon the ratio between the amount of labor seeking employment and the capital devoted to its employment, then high wages, the mark of the relative scarcity of labor, must be accompanied by low interest, the mark of the relative abundance of capital, and conversely, low wages must be accompanied by high interest.

This, according to George, is not the fact; but the contrary is always true. Where wages are high interest is high. In our own era, observing several business cycles, the intelligent observer need not be a political economist to see that brisk times calling for greater numbers of workers and higher wages are always accompanied by high rates of interest making available the capital to engage this larger number of workers. Isn't it a fact that where high economic activity, with its increasing demand for capital, thereby raising interest rates, causes governmental authority to fear accelerating inflation, it acts to restrict credit by requiring greater bank reserves, thus slowing down business activity by the dearth of affordable credit? Then, after inflation eases, the Federal Reserve resets interest rates low to maintain or stimulate business activity.

George then proceeded to present many examples to show that the concept of the "wages fund" was sheer nonsense, a mere assumption which, upon but little examination, contradicted the apparent facts. Drawing upon a false premise with sound reasoning had produced a false conclusion.

George then proceeded to present, instead, the following (revolutionary) proposition: "that wages, instead of being drawn from capital, are in reality drawn from the product of the labor for which they are paid." This proposition is fleshed out in detail later, but in the meantime, he demonstrated that the demolition of the "wages" fund theory reduced to rubble the entire edifice of his contemporaneous political economy, with all of its ramifications, namely:

a. that industry is limited by capital;

b. that capital must be accumulated before labor is employed, and labor cannot be employed except as capital is accumulated;

c. the doctrine that every increase of capital gives, or is capable of giving, additional employment to industry;

d. the doctrine that the conversion of circulating capital into fixed capital lessens the fund applicable to labor;

e. the doctrine that more laborers can be employed at low than high wages.

It must be pointed out that even to this day, discredited and superseded as the "wages fund" in fact is, reference is continually made by economists, in respected economic journals, to the observation that a certain specific amount of capital must be present, or made available, for the creation of each and every job in industry. But these capital funds, augmented by generous depreciation allowances, do not necessarily translate to wages, despite persistent tax cut incentives to industries operating at, say, eighty percent of full capacity.

George continued his refutation of the now discredited "wages fund" theory as follows:

"Yet, in the very treatises in which the limitation of industry by capital is laid down without reservation and made the basis for the most important reasonings and theories, we are told that capital is stored-up or accumulated labor—"that part of wealth which is saved to assist further production." If we substitute for the word "capital" this definition of the word, the proposition carries its own refutation, for that labor cannot be employed until the results of labor are saved becomes too absurd for discussion."

George now proceeded by numerous examples to demonstrate that society in its most highly developed form is but an elaboration of society in its modest beginnings, and that principles obvious in the simpler relations of men and women are merely disguised and not abrogated or reversed by the more intricate relations that result from the division of labor and the use of complex tools and methods. He then continued to establish by these examples the claim that each specialist producer may rightly demand a proportionate share of all production toward which he has in fact contributed.

In order to guarantee the certainty of his prior deductive reasoning from principles, George asserted that he would proceed from the facts to arrive at the principles he had previously asserted, by means of inductive reasoning. It may now be seen by the studious reader that the towering edifice of political economy which George would erect required the demolition and removal of elaborated, conventionally accepted falsehoods bearing much resemblance to those required to buttress the Ptolemaic theory of the earth's centrality to the visible solar system.

2

UNAMBIGUOUS DEFINITIONS OF TERMS

George now continued his inquiry by undertaking to define the terms commonly used in written and spoken discussions of political economy. He pointed out that terms such as "wealth," "capital," "rent," and "wages," have been, and were in his time, given significantly varying definitions, therefore leading to differing and confusing conclusions by the most eminent of political economists.

As regards the term "wages," there has been given a sufficiently definite meaning by economic writers from the outset. Wages are paid to someone who is employed by someone else, and may be contrasted with one who works for himself. There has been little disagreement in defining "wages" as payment for a hired hand, both among economic writers as well as in general usage.

However, in political economy the word "wages" has a much wider meaning, and includes all return for exertion. As political economists explain, the three factors of production are land, labor, and capital, and that part of production which goes to the second of these factors is by them termed "wages."

Thus the term "wages" includes all human exertion in the production of wealth; and wages, being that part of production which goes to labor, includes all rewards for such exertion. There is then in the politico—economic sense of the term "wages" no distinction as to the kind of labor, whether it is received through an employer or not; but "wages" means the return for the exertion of labor, as distinguished from the return received for the use of capital, and the return received by the landholder for the use of his land.

While the sense of the term wages is recognized with greater or lesser clarity, it is not so in the case of capital. In general discourse, all sorts of things that have a value, or will yield a return, are vaguely spoken of as capital, while economic writers, certainly in George's time, differed so widely that the term hardly could be said to have a fixed meaning.

Adam Smith's definition of capital includes, among several terms which will be seen to meet George's concise and precise definition, such items as "the acquired and useful abilities of all the inhabitants, and money." It may readily be seen that "acquired and useful abilities…" more readily find themselves as a component of labor; and "money," in and of itself, say as lunch money in the pocket of a working man (or a banker, for that matter) can hardly be seen as yielding a return other than sustenance, once spent.

Ricardo's definition of capital differs widely from Adam Smith's by omitting numerous factors cited by Smith, and by the inclusion of "food and clothing" as being necessary to "give effect to labor."

John Stuart Mill's definition of capital makes neither the use nor capability of use, but the determination to use, the test of capital. "Whatever things are destined to supply productive labor with the shelter, protection, tools and materials which the work requires, and to feed and otherwise maintain the laborer during the process, are capital."

It is interesting to note in Mill's definition an inadvertent obeisance to the "wages fund" theory in referring to the need to provide productive labor with shelter, protection, and food to maintain the laborer during the process. Tools and materials which the work requires are here lumped in with the return to labor for exertion; and the laborer's requirements for sustenance are of concern only as he participates in wealth production.

Generally, people understand what capital is until they begin to define the term. It is widely comprehended that capital is that part of wealth which is intended to generate more wealth, and that with certain assets there exists an ambiguity because these assets may at one time be simply evidence of wealth, and at other times objects of exchange for the purpose of realizing profit, that is, more wealth. As an example, jewelry about the neck of the jeweler's wife will simply be evidence of his wealth, while jewelry for sale in his shop is certainly his capital; and should circumstances permit or require him to sell his wife's jewelry, wealth is thereby converted to capital.

It is necessary to exclude from the category of capital anything that may be included in the categories of either land or labor. Doing so, there remain only things which are neither land nor labor, but which have resulted from the union of these two factors of production. Nothing can be properly capital that does not consist of these—that is to say, nothing can be capital that is not wealth.

As commonly used, the word "wealth" is applied to anything having an exchange value. But when used as a term of political economy, it must be limited to a much more definite meaning, because many things are commonly spoken of as wealth which, in taking account of collective or general wealth, cannot be considered as wealth at all.

Such things have an exchange value, and are commonly spoken of as wealth, inasmuch as they represent as between individuals or sets of individuals, the power of obtaining wealth, since their increase or decrease does not affect the sum of wealth. Such are bonds, mortgages, promissory notes, bank bills, or other stipulations for the transfer of wealth. Increase in the amount of bonds, mortgages, notes or bank bills cannot increase the wealth of the community that includes as well those who promise to pay as those who are entitled to receive.

Everything that has an exchange value is, therefore, not wealth, in the only sense in which the term can be used in political economy. Only such things can be wealth the production of which increases, and the destruction of which decreases, the aggregate wealth. Thus wealth, as alone the term can be used in political economy, consists of natural products that have been secured, moved, combined, separated, or in other ways modified by human exertion so as to fit them for the gratification of human desire. Nothing which nature supplies to man without his labor is wealth, nor does the expenditure of labor result in wealth unless there is a tangible product which has and retains the power of ministering to desire.

Although all capital is wealth, not all wealth is capital. Capital is only a part of wealth—that part, namely, which is devoted to the aid of production. Adam Smith, a man of the highest talents, never-the-less described "personal qualities" among his list of items qualifying as capital, an inclusion which is not consistent with his original definition of capital as stock from which revenue is expected. Clearly, much confusion over the subject prevailed among the highest academic personalities. Today, among many academics and the vast majority of thinking persons, the same confusion exists and is often deliberately disseminated.

After separating the wealth that is capital from the wealth that is not capital, and looking for the distinction, we shall not find it to be in the character, capabilities, or final destination of the things themselves, but as to whether or not they pass into the possession of the consumer.

The reader will surely be surprised to learn that paper money (unlike gold or silver specie) is not wealth, and therefore cannot be capital. It may, however, not unlike any scrip, lay claim to wealth.

Now, capital, in being wealth devoted to production, requires that the definition of production be expanded, not only to making things, but the bringing of them to the consumer.

3

THE TRUE SOURCES OF WAGES

Seeking to utterly impeach the doctrine that capital, by its quantity and nature, determines the employment and wages of labor, George proceed to show that labor, in effect and reality, pays its own wages in the value it adds to basic natural substances or natural substances partially worked up into capital by labor beforehand.

These early arguments, in George's view, are necessary to clear the ground for the new political economy which he is prepared to seed with an entirely new doctrine—one which accurately establishes the actual distribution of product to the three factors of production.

In all those cases in which the laborer is his own employer and takes directly the produce of his labor as its reward, it is plain enough that wages are not drawn from capital, but result directly in the product of his labor. If, for instance, the laborer devotes his labor to gathering birds' eggs or picking wild berries, the eggs or berries he thus gets are his wages. Surely, no one will contend that in such a case wages are drawn from capital. There is no capital in the case. An absolutely naked man thrown on an island where no human being has trod before, may gather birds' eggs or berries, which constitute his wages.

If a workman takes a piece of leather and works it up into a pair of shoes, the shoes are his wage—the reward of his exertion. Surely, they are not drawn from capital—his capital or anyone else's capital—but are brought into existence by the labor by which they become the wages, and in obtaining this pair of shoes as the wages of his labor, capital is not even momentarily lessened one iota.

Adam Smith, who gave the direction to economic thought that has resulted in the current elaborated theories of the relation between wages and capital, recognized the fact that in such simple cases as has been instanced, wages are the product of labor (Chapter VIII)[1]*. He wrote:

"The produce of labor constitutes the natural recompense or wages of labor. In that original state of things which precede the appropriation of land and the accumulation of stock, the whole produce of labor belongs to the laborer. He has neither landlord nor master to share with him."

Adam Smith then proceeded to forget the truth of the initial conditions and relationships and advanced his theoretical constructions by assuming that the master is considered as providing from his capital the wages of his workmen.

George does not venture to suggest an intellectual lapse on the part of Adam Smith, nor a prejudice in favor of the class of landowners and new industrialists to whom he was, in fact, beholden for his high position in academia and for the many honors bestowed on him.

George, instead of casting aspersions on the honored political economist, proceeded to build his argument upon Smith's original perception.

Next to the simplicity of "that original state of things," of which many examples could still be found, was the arrangement in which the laborer, through working for another person, received his wages in kind— that is to say, in the things his labor produced.

The farming of land on shares (share-cropping), which prevailed to a considerable extent in the southern states of the Union and in

---

1   *The Wealth of Nations

California, the metayer system of Europe, as well as the many cases in which superintendents, salesmen, etc. were paid by a percentage of gross income or profits, what were they but the employment of labor for wages which consisted of part of its produce?

The next step in the advance from simplicity to complexity is where wages, though estimated in kind, are paid in an equivalent of something else. For instance, on American whaling ships the custom was not to pay fixed wages, but a "lay," or proportion of the catch, which varied from a sixteenth to a twelfth to the captain, down to a three-hundredth to the cabin boy. Thus, when a whale ship came into New Bedford or San Francisco after a successful cruise, she carried in her hold the wages of her crew, as well as the profits of her owners, and an equivalence which would reimburse them for all the stores used up during the voyage. Could anything be clearer than that these wages—this oil and bone which the crew of the whaler had taken—have not been drawn from capital, but are really a part of the produce of their labor?

Admiralty law lends credence to the proposition that production is always the mother of wages, in that the loss of freight due to disaster at sea, which prevents a ship from earning on the delivery of freight, deprives the seaman of his legal claim to wages. Without production, wages could not be, independently of capital invested. It is from the produce of labor, not from the advances of capital that wages come.

George dwelled upon the obvious fact that labor always preceded wages because it was all-important to an understanding of the more complicated phenomena of wages.

In clarification of the appearance that the employer reduces his capital to the extent that he pays out wages (as well as other charges against production), George asserted:

"And as the employer generally makes a profit, the pay of wages is, so far as he is concerned, but the return to the laborer of the portion of the capital he has received from the labor. So far as the employee is concerned, it is but the receipt of a portion of the capital his labor has previously produced..."

Capital has never to be set aside for the payment of wages when the produce of the labor is exchanged as soon as it is produced;

it is only required when this product is stored up, or what is to the individual the same thing, placed in the general current of exchanges without being at once drawn against—that is, sold on credit. But the capital thus required is not required for the payment of wages, nor for advances to labor. It is never as an employer of labor that any producer needs capital; when he does need capital, it is because he is not only an employer of labor, but a merchant or speculator in, or an accumulator of, the products of labor.

4

CAPITAL VERSUS WEALTH

So preoccupied was Henry George with successfully storming the hitherto impregnable fortress of the "wages fund," buttressed by the repugnant Malthusian theory of ever-increasing population growth requiring either moral or murderous restraint, that he felt it necessary to cap his prior arguments with a carefully structured dismemberment of the ancillary doctrine suggesting that the maintenance of labor depended upon capital, not on the product of present labor.

The doctrine was expressed as follows:

"Population regulates itself by the funds which are to employ it, and therefore always increases or diminishes with the increase or diminution of capital."

George regarded such reasoning as absurd, for it involved the idea that labor cannot be exerted until the products of labor are saved—thus putting the product before the producer. To assert that because food, raiment, and shelter are necessary to productive labor, therefore industry is limited by capital, is to ignore the distinction between capital and wealth, which latter category, in modest quantity, will exist even in the laborer's household, of sufficient quantity to feed, clothe, and shelter his family for a short time.

But, though it would be logically sufficient, it is hardly safe, in George's view, to rest there and leave the argument to hinge on the distinction between wealth and capital. He therefore pursued the larger argument that, before a work which will not immediately result in wealth available for subsistence can be carried on, there must exist such a stock of subsistence as will support the laborers during the process.

He insisted that it is not necessary to the production of things that cannot be used as subsistence, or be immediately utilized, that there should have been a previous production of the wealth required for the maintenance of the laborers while the production is going on. It is only necessary that there should be somewhere within the circle of exchange a contemporaneous production of sufficient subsistence exchangeable for the thing upon which the labor is being bestowed.

Is it not true, George asked rhetorically, that in any normal condition of things consumption is supported by contemporaneous production?

He offers the telling example of a luxurious idler who does no productive work, but lives upon the wealth his father left him, securely invested in government bonds.

"On his table are new-laid eggs, butter churned but a few days before, milk which the cow gave this morning, fish which twenty-four hours ago were swimming in the sea, meat which the butcher boy has just brought in time to be cooked, vegetables fresh from the garden and fruit from the orchard...In short, there is hardly anything which has not recently left the hand of the productive laborer (in this category must be included transporters and distributors as well as those engaged in the first stages of production). What this man inherited from his father, and on which we say he lives, is not actually wealth at all, but only the power of commanding wealth as others produce it. And it is from contemporaneous production that his subsistence is drawn.

The principle that "The demand for consumption determines the direction in which labor will be expended thus articulates how completely true it is that, in whatever is taken or consumed by laborers in return for labor rendered, there is no advance of capital to the laborers. As a matter of fact, where there is labor looking for employment, the want of capital does not prevent the owner of land which promises a crop for which there is a demand from hiring it. Either he makes an agreement to cultivate on shares, or if he prefers to pay wages, the farmer himself will obtain credit, and thus the work done in cultivation is immediately utilized or exchanged for as it is done."

A few words by the author of this work appear to be in order now. The diligent reader will surely have noted that several of the examples either quoted previously from Henry George's work or alluded to without quotation, have a decided nineteenth century context or flavor. The reader is implored not to reject the current relevance of the meanings intended by the examples, and recall that the purpose of this inquiry is not only to confirm George's vision, but to establish its current and future relevance. An assault upon a heavily fortified, long-standing conventional (but untrue) doctrine requires an extremely careful mobilization of facts and examples before proceeding with the actual assault upon a redoubt previously considered impregnable.

The truths, both Henry George's as well as the author's elaboration and projection of politico-economic reality, will more than compensate, in the author's view, for the somewhat difficult and tedious journey to that goal.

5

THE TRUE ROLE OF CAPITAL

George then raised the rhetorical question:

"If capital is not required for the payment of wages during production, what then are its functions?"

He answered the question directly:

"Capital consists of wealth used for the procurement of more wealth, as distinguished from wealth used for the direct satisfaction of desire; or it (capital) may be defined as wealth in the course of exchange."

Capital, therefore, increases the power of labor to produce wealth by:

1. enabling labor to avail itself more efficiently of the reproductive forces of nature,

2. permitting the division of labor, and

3. enabling labor to apply itself in more effective ways.

Capital does not supply the materials which labor works up into wealth; the materials of wealth are supplied by nature. But such materials partially worked up and in the course of exchange are capital.

Capital does not limit industry, as is erroneously taught, the only limit to industry being the access to natural material.

But capital may limit the form of industry and the productivity of industry by limiting the use of tools and the division of labor.

To say that capital may limit the form of industry or the productivity of industry is a very different thing than saying that capital limits industry. For the dictum of George's contemporaneous political economy (as well as many political economists today, that "capital limits industry") meant not that capital limits the form or productivity of industry, but that it limits the exertion of labor.

In many backward and impoverished countries which might experience greater productivity and well being by the accretion of domestic capital, it is not actually the lack of capital, but the depredations and abuses of government, the insecurity of property, and the ignorance and prejudice of the people that prevent the accumulation and use of capital.

The introduction, benefits, and abuses of foreign capital is a subject requiring independent examination.

Although there may be in a community individuals who, from want of capital, cannot apply their labor as efficiently as they would care to, yet so long as there is a sufficiency of capital in the community at large, the real limitation is not the lack of capital, but the want of its proper distribution.

George persisted: "It is not from any scarcity of capital that the poverty of the masses in civilized countries proceeds. For not only do wages nowhere reach the limit fixed by the productiveness of industry, but wages are *relatively* the lowest where capital is most abundant."

We begin to see here a situation analogous to the one previously described, where the percentile of productivity withheld from rent shrinks, must shrink, but the absolute quantity may remain the same or rise above historical levels. This phenomenon and its significance will be examined later.

To recapitulate, as George does: "We have seen that the current theory that wages depend upon the ratio between the number of laborers and the amount of capital devoted to the employment of labor is inconsistent with the general fact that wages and interest do not rise and fall inversely, but co-jointly.

"The discrepancy having led us to an examination of the grounds of the theory, we have seen further that contrary to the current idea, wages are not drawn from capital at all, but come directly from the produce of the labor for which they are paid. We have seen that capital does not advance wages or subsist laborers, but that its functions are to assist labor with tools, seeds, etc., and with the wealth required to carry on exchanges.

"We are thus irresistibly led to practical conclusion so important as to justify the pains taken to make sure."

"For if wages are drawn, not from capital, but from the produce of labor, THE CURRENT THEORIES AS TO THE RELATIONS OF CAPITAL AND LABOR ARE INVALID, AND ALL REMEDIES BY PROFESSORS OF POLITICAL ECONOMY EITHER BY THE INCREASE OF CAPITAL, OR THE RESTRICTION OF THE NUMBER OF LABORERS, OR THE EFFICIENY OF THEIR WORK MUST BE CONDEMNED."

Since each laborer in performing the labor really creates the fund from which his wages are drawn, then wages cannot be diminished by the increase of laborers. It is this which raises the question, presumptively, of the productive powers of nature tending to decrease with the increasing demands made of them by increasing population.

6

THE MALTHUSIAN THEORY IMPEACHED

Behind and buttressing the theory of the "wages fund" (the demolition of which was so crucial to George's further inquiry) was the Malthusian theory, a doctrine which stipulated that population naturally tended to increase faster than subsistence.

These two doctrines, fitting with each other, according to George, were the pillars supporting the contemporary political economy like a towering fortress obscuring and defending the status quo against rational analysis of the great problem he was endeavoring to solve. The prevailing theory of wages had never been fairly put on trial because, backed by the Malthusian theory, it seemed to the minds of political economists a self-evident truth.

These two theories mutually blended with, strengthened, and defended each other, while they both derived additional support brought forward in the discussions of the theory of rent - viz., that past a certain point the application of capital and labor to land yields a diminishing return. Together, they gave such an explanation of the phenomena as seemed to fit all the facts.

The Malthusian doctrine may be stated in its strongest and least objectionable form as follows:

"Population, constantly tending to increase, must, when unrestrained, ultimately press against the limits of subsistence, not as against a fixed, but as against an elastic barrier, which makes the procurement of subsistence progressively more and more difficult. And thus, where reproduction has had time to assert its power, and is unchecked by prudence, there must exist that degree of want which will keep population within the bounds of subsistence."

The great cause of the triumph of this theory, despite its many illogicalities and vulnerabilities was that, instead of menacing any vested right or antagonizing any powerful interest, it was eminently soothing and reassuring to the classes who, wielding the power of wealth, largely dominated thought. At a time when old supports were falling away, it came to the rescue of the special privileges by which a few monopolized so much of the good things of the world, proclaiming a natural cause for the want and misery which, if attributed to political institutions, would condemn every government under which they exist.

The combination of the theory of the "wages fund," the Malthusian doctrine, and Ricardo's observation that rising population must increase rent as less productive lands are necessarily required to be put into production, ensured that any reforms which would interfere with the interest of any powerful class would be discouraged as hopeless.

Nevertheless, as George perceived that the contemporary theory of the "wages fund" had been successfully overthrown, he felt certain that he could overthrow its twin, the Malthusian theory.

George then proceeded to demolish the Malthusian theory factually and by analogy, by compelling arguments which will not be repeated here, except for one amusing analysis regarding the Chinese Philosopher Confucius.

According to George, the descendants of Confucius still existed in China at the time of his writing, and enjoyed particular privileges and consideration, in fact forming the only hereditary aristocracy. On the presumption that population tends to double every twenty-five years, (Malthus's assertion), they should, in 2,150 years after the death of Confucius, have amounted to 859,559,193,106,709,670,198,528 souls. Instead of any such unimaginable number, the descendants of Confucius, 2,150 years after his death, in the reign of Kanghi, numbered 11,000 males, say 22,000 souls. So much for geometric increase.

In our own era, the new twenty-first century, the fact is that sustenance is generally most abundant where the population density is highest, and where hunger prevails, other than in consequence of warfare or other emergent circumstances, it is a consequence of the inability to pay, rather than a deficiency of available nutriments.

As an example, in India and China, where famine and widespread starvation have often prevailed in the past when their populations, while large, were smaller than they presently are, there is currently very little report of hunger. Does this not suggest that factors other than population size influence available sustenance?

7

THE DISTRIBUTION OF WEALTH

It was now clearly established by George that, in spite of the enormous increase of productive wealth, the great body of workers were provided with the least part of the product upon which they would consent to live. It had also been clearly established that it was not the limitations of nature which contributed to the phenomenon stated above. That being the case, George determined to move from consideration of the factors which bounded the production of wealth to seek the laws which governed its distribution.

Such readers as may be inclined to believe that the paradox described previously and above was confined to the era in which George lived should consider the following:

The wealth of the Forbes 400 richest Americans grew an average of $1.44 billion each year from 1997-2000, for an average daily increase of wealth of $1,920,000 per person. That was 6,602 times the minimum wage;

The top fifth of U.S. households had 49.2% of the national income, while the bottom fifth got by on 3.6%.

The financial wealth of the top one percent of U.S. households in 2002 exceeded the combined household wealth of the bottom 95%.

The relevance of George's findings almost 125 years ago to current circumstances will be established later in this work, although his inquiry was largely confined to the depredations of rent upon overall production. We are as yet newly embarked on our inquiry into both George's amazing insights and their extension and elaboration into the present.

To quote George:

"It will be necessary to review in its main branches the whole subject of the distribution of wealth. To discover the cause which, as population increases and the productive arts advance, deepens the poverty of the lowest class, we must find the law which determines what part of the produce is distributed to labor as wages. To find the law of wages, or at least to make sure when we have found it, we must determine the laws which fix the part of the produce which goes to capital and the part which goes to landowners, for as land, labor, and capital join in producing wealth, it is between these three that the produce must be divided.

"As I have already explained, production does not merely mean the making of things, but includes the increase of value gained by transporting or exchanging things."

George goes on to assert that the correlation of the three factors of production was not, and could not be achieved previously because of the incompatibility of the varied definitions of the term capital by the contemporaneous political economy with the definitions of the two other factors of production.

Rent, as traditionally defined, expressed the return to the owners of land. Wages clearly enough expressed the return to labor

But the third term—that which expressed the return to capital, was, in the standard works, beset with a puzzling degree of ambiguity and confusion.

"In common speech, the term which came closest to expressing the return for the use of capital was interest, exclusive of any labor, management, or risk, except as may be involved in the security itself. The word profit was almost synonymous with revenue, meaning gain, an amount in excess of expenditure, and frequently included receipts which were properly wages, as well as for the risk peculiar to the various uses of capital. That being the case, the term profit necessarily required that its classically defined components, wages of superintendence, compensation for risk, and interest be distributed among the three compensations for the factors of production, rent, wages, and interest." It was now clearly established by George that, in spite of the enormous increase of productive wealth, the great body of workers were provided with the least part of the product upon which they would consent to live. It had also been clearly established that it was not the limitations of nature which contributed to the phenomenon stated above. That being the case, George determined to move from consideration of the factors which bounded the production of wealth to seek the laws which governed its distribution.

George pointed out that much of the uncovered error in the prevailing political economy of his time was rooted in the perception of capital as the prime mover in generating wealth. The capitalist was seen as renting land and hiring labor to begin the process of production.

Looking upon capital as the employer of labor led to the theory that wages depended upon the relative abundance of capital and to the theory that interest varied inversely with wages.

But when the origin and natural sequence of things is considered, the order is reversed; and capital, instead of being first, is last, and is in fact employed by labor. Labor can be exerted upon land, and it is from land that the matter that it transforms to wealth must be drawn. Land is therefore the preceding condition, the field and material of labor. The material order is land, labor, capital; and instead of starting from capital as the initial point, the start should be with land.

Another significant insight of George's is that capital is not a necessary factor in production. Labor exerted upon land can produce wealth without the aid of capital, and in the necessary genesis of things, must produce wealth before capital can exist. Therefore, the law of rent and the law of wages must correlate with each other and form a perfect whole without reference to the law of capital, as otherwise these laws would not fit the cases, which could readily be imagined, and which to some degree actually existed, in which capital took no part in production.

And as capital is, as was so often said, but stored up labor, it is but a form of labor, and its law could only be subordinate to, and independently correlative with, the law of wages, so as to fit the cases where the whole product is divided between labor and capital, without any deduction for rent.

There are undoubtedly those readers who will find it difficult, if not impossible, within our present economic culture, to accept the concept of capital not being the initiator in activities leading to the production of wealth. While the author at this point is dealing with theoretical concepts, as did George at this stage of his inquiry, and will address this issue in greater detail subsequently, he wishes to remind the reader that capital, by its very nature, is risk averse, and urges him or her to reflect upon the distinction between capitalist, entrepreneur, and pro-active government in this regard.

If one were to consult the financial pages of a responsible newspaper, one would observe the enormous debt carried by the most successful and venerable corporations. This debt (in the form of bonds) is generally held by institutions such as banks and insurance companies and represents conservative, highly collateralized capital. Where institutions and wealthy individuals hold stock, it must be remembered that these securities, in the true sense of the word, are not wealth (so they cannot be capital), as they have little or no claim on the capital of the company.

When investment banking houses underwrite securities issued for an enterprise, they will generally accept a large block of shares as part of their fee for placing those shares among the public, while establishing themselves in a favorable position to underwrite bond sales to other institutions and wealthy individuals who, like themselves, demand tangible collateral as well as seats on the boards of such companies.

Capital does not initiate except where government guarantees investment. Inventors assisted by entrepreneurs exercising consider-able human exertion (labor) and by exposing themselves to genuine risk (supposedly the justification for profit) are the initiators.

We shall now leave this issue aside for the time being.

8

THE NATURE OF "LAND"

In pursuit of the goal of his inquiry, that of determining why the return to labor generally shrinks even in a period of robust enhancement of production, George began with an analysis of the basis for rent.

Having established the basis for rent, the basis for wages and interest combined could readily be calculated; and where no capital was involved, the basis for wages, the return to labor, could be deduced.

It is worth noting that George made reference to "owners of land or OTHER NATURAL CAPABILITIES" in the same breath, thereby expanding the range of the first factor of production—all the planet's natural endowments—beyond the definition of his traditional predecessors. He described rent as follows:

"Rent, in short, is a share in the wealth produced which the exclusive right to the use of natural capabilities gives to the owner. Rent may be real or it may be potential, and it does not justify its participation in the fruits of overall production by help or advantage given to production. It is valueless without the application of labor, real or potential, and receives its share simply through a monopolistic capacity of refusal."

George now began to lay down the foundation for the rational computation of rent by the observation that privately owned land will yield no rent when land of equal value can be had without cost. When free land is fully appropriated, or is inferior in fertility, then the land of higher quality with greater real or potential capacity becomes marginally more valuable, and may command rent proportionately.

Rent, therefore is possible and reasonable because land or other natural capabilities are not uniformly endowed, and because they are privately owned.

Where certain natural capabilities cannot be privately owned, such as the Grand Banks fishing zone, there can be no rent, and labor and capital alone share the fruits of production.

If all the land of a community is owned by a single potentate, as has frequently been the case throughout history, he could, and did, order groups and individuals to depart, even to perish thereby. The term "real estate," in essence, describes all the land of some nations as essentially being "the royal estate," namely, the kings, with varying rights of tenancy and circumscribed possession.

Others, before George, had established that the rent of land was determined by the excess of its produce over that which the same application of labor and capital could secure from the least productive land in use. However, none before George utilized this knowledge in pursuing its coordination with the laws of wages and interest—and certainly not with George's motivation for his inquiry.

George expressed the relationship between the three factors of production thusly in order to elaborate upon the law of rent:

Produce = Rent + Wages + Interest

Therefore; Produce - Rent = Wages + Interest

"Thus wages and interest do not depend upon the produce of labor and capital, but upon what is left after rent is taken out, or upon the produce which they could obtain without paying rent—that is, from the poorest land in use. And hence, no matter what be the increase in productive power, if the increase in rent keep up with it, neither wages nor capital can increase," George wrote.

"The moment this simple relationship is recognized, one can see at once why wages and interest fail to increase with increase of productive power; rent sweeps away all that is above the 'rent line.'

"Thus, where the value of land is low, there may be a small production of wealth, and yet a high rate of wages and interest, as in new countries. And where the value of land is high, there may be a very large production of wealth, and yet a low rate of wages and interest."

If the value of land increases faster than productive power, rent will swallow up even more than the increase; and while the product of labor and capital will be much larger, wages and interest will fall. It is only when the value of land fails to increase as rapidly as productive powers that wages and interest can increase with the increase of productive power. All this is exemplified by actual experience—up until the present time, particularly if one observes "the cartelized rent" demanded by the international owners of energy resources in the guise of national states.

9

THE LAW OF INTEREST

In pursuit of his ultimate goal, determination of the law of wages, George chose to digress from direct pursuit to an analysis of the law of interest, inasmuch as, having enunciated and then establishing the law of interest, the law of wages could readily be laid bare. He explained that digression as a means of dispelling the view that interest, the return to capital, is unnatural, unjustified, and a hindrance to economic and social justice.

George stressed that interest, as an abstract term in the distribution of wealth, differs in meaning from the word as commonly used. It includes all return for the use of capital, not merely those that pass from borrower to lender, and excludes compensation for risk, which forms so great a part of what is commonly called interest. What he sought to discover is what fixes the general rate of interest proper. The different rates of compensation for risk added to this provides the current rate of commercial interest. He also pointed out, in previously discussing prevailing political economic theories, that contemporaneous understanding of interest in relation to the availability of capital and labor were entirely in error.

George then raised the rhetorical question: what is the justification for interest? In pursuit of the answer, he examined a most respected theory, that of Bastiat's, examining his oft-quoted illustration of the plane, and found it deficient, concluding that, "If 'the power exists in tools to increase the productiveness of labor' were the cause of interest, then the rate of interest would increase with the march of invention. This is not so. The improvement of tools does not add to reproductive power of capital; it adds to the reproductive power of labor."

George now introduced a concept he called the active power of nature, the principle of growth, of reproduction, though generally requiring some labor, yet separable and distinct from labor. He expressed the belief that it is this phenomenon which is the cause of interest, or the increase of capital over and above that due to labor.

As examples of this phenomenon, he pointed to wine put away and improving over time without much of labor's intervention; the same with the reproductive capacity of cattle, bees, seeds, etc. It was the interchangeability of wealth through the entire circle of production which transmitted this particular increase of capital to a community's overall store. "Were the quality and capacity of matter everywhere uniform," George wrote, "and all productive power in man, there would be no interest." George further stated, on the issue of interest: "Thus, interest springs from the power of increase which the reproductive forces of nature, and the in effect analogous capacity for exchange, give to capital. It is not arbitrary, but a natural thing; it is not the result of a particular social organization, but the laws of the universe which underlie society. It is therefore just."

In a remarkable feat of deductive reasoning, George employed the previously formulated equation:

Produce—Rent = Wages + Interest
to show that the law of interest correlates directly (but inversely) with the law of rent.

It is necessary first to imagine "a fool's paradise," as Carlyle called it, where the production of wealth went on without the aid of labor (that the trend to the replacement of workers in production with "intelligent machines" proceeds in just that direction, the perceptive reader will already acknowledge), depending solely upon the "active reproductive power of nature" alone.

It may be seen that the rate of interest thereby would be determined by the return to capital upon the poorest land in which capital is freely applied—that is to say, upon the best land open to it without the payment of rent.

In Carlyle's example, where rent increases as the margin of cultivation extends further and further out until it is, theoretically, capable of consuming all product, so will it diminish the right side of the equation containing only interest to zero, theoretically. Interest, consequently, must decrease as rent increases.

10

THE RELATIONSHIP OF THE FACTORS OF PRODUCTION

Examining the previously referenced equation relating the three factors of production, we may now allow capital to approach zero as a limit, reflecting a real world situation where only labor impresses itself upon matter without the help of capital. Numerous examples could be shown, and are given in George's work, but will not be repeated here.

It should immediately be apparent that, if rent increases, and approaches the value of the entire production, labor, theoretically, could be excluded from any return.

Of course, as a practical matter, the elimination of all return to labor would cause the entire system of production to break down, with laborers starved or displaced and landowners bereft of any production. Such dramatic and unreasonable a state of affairs would also be unlikely to occur due to the competition of various landowners and their recognition of their best interests.

However, that "margin of production," where rent absorbs all production except for the quantity required to maintain the life and reproductive capacity of labor, was described by Ricardo and Smith as "the point of natural wages."

Consequently, as described by George, "The law of wages depends upon the margin of production, or upon the product which labor can obtain at the highest point of natural productivity open to it without the payment of rent."

It can be seen that the law of wages, like that of interest, is a corollary (but inversely) of the law of rent, as can be observed by manipulation of, first one, and then the other, factor on the right hand side of the previously referenced equation.

The law of wages accords with and explains universal facts that, without its understanding, seem unrelated and contradictory. It shows that:

(a) where land is free and labor is unassisted by capital the whole product will go to labor as wages

(b) where land is free and labor is assisted by capital, wages will consist of the whole product less that part necessary to induce the storing up of labor as capital

(c) where land is subject to ownership, and rent arises, wages will be fixed by what labor could secure from the highest natural opportunity open to it without the payment of rent

(d) where natural opportunities are monopolized, wages may be forced by the competition among laborers to the minimum at which laborers will consent to reproduce.

The accepted law of rent, in fact, depends for its recognition upon a previous, though it seems in many cases to be an unconscious, acceptance of the law of wages. What makes it evident that land of a particular quality yields as rent the surplus of its produce over that of the least productive land in use is comprehension of the fact that the owner of the higher quality land can procure the labor to work his land by the payment of what that same labor can procure from land of poorer quality.

One man will not work for another for less than his labor will really yield when he can go upon the next quarter section and take up a farm for himself. It is only as land became monopolized, and these natural opportunities were shut off from labor, that laborers were required to compete with each other for employment. It then became possible for the farmer to hire hands to do his work while he maintained himself on the difference between what their labor produced and what he paid them for it.

As regards the classical political economists who preceded George, it is difficult to resist the impression that some of them really saw this law of wages, but fearful of the practical consequences to which it would lead, preferred to ignore and cover it up, rather than use it as the key to the problems which, without it, are so perplexing.

If the margin of cultivation descends from the productive point which we will call 25, to the productive point we will call 20, the rent of all lands that before paid rent will increase by this difference, and the proportion of the whole produce which goes to laborers as wages, will to the same extent diminish; but if, in the meantime, the advance of the arts or the economics that become possible with greater population have so increased the productive power of labor that at 20 the same exertion will produce as much wealth as before at 25, laborers will get as wages as great a quantity as before, and the relative fall of wages will not be noticeable in any diminution of the necessities or comforts of the laborer, but only in the increased value of land.

The reader is reminded that the reference to "land" is to all of "nature's natural endowments," none of which can be created by man (or woman). As the early development of the subject of political economy occurred in an era where almost all wealth derived from agriculture, the terminology and examples, both of the early political economists and necessarily, George himself, were either exclusively or primarily couched in agricultural terms.

However, it will subsequently be shown that the laws of rent, interest, and wages apply as much today, in our post-industrial era, as they did prior to their formulation by Henry George in 1879.

In fact, it is the purpose of this work, as previously stated, to endorse, amend where necessary, and to extend the mighty insights of Henry George's inquiry into the twenty-first century.

Again, patience is requested of the gentle reader, who will surely be rewarded for it as he reads on.

11

RENT, WAGES, AND INTEREST CORRELATED

George now dwelt upon the correlation of the laws of rent, wages, and interest, which he contrasted with the incoherence of the explanations and definitions of the various maxims of his contemporaneous political economy.

Before proceeding to contrast the then current laws of political economy with those which he derived, George emphasized the importance of understanding the pivotal role of competition among laborers making possible the operation of the law of rent and its corollaries. It was the competition among laborers which made possible the same payment for labor on superior as well as on inferior lands, and the operation of the line of cultivation and the law of rent.

George spoke to this as follows:

"For on what depends the recognition of the law of rent? Evidently upon the recognition of the fact that the effect of competition is to prevent the return to labor and capital being anywhere greater than upon the poorest land in use. It is in seeing this that we see the owner of land will be able to claim as rent all of the produce which exceeds what would be yielded to an equal application of labor and capital on the poorest land in use."

This statement, however, raises a perplexing question or two regarding the linkage of labor and capital where the statement would be both clearer and more accurate devoid of the mention of capital. Surely, the competition of which he wrote was applicable solely to that of laborers, yet labor and capital are linked in describing the depredations imposed by the application of the law of rent. This tendency on George's part will be addressed subsequently in greater detail.

Meanwhile, the comparisons of the old and new political economy:

The Current Statement(1879)	The true statement
Rent depends on the margin of cultivation, rising as it falls and falling as it rises	Rent depends on the margin of cultivation, rising as it falls and falling as it rises
Wages depend upon the ratio between the number of laborers and the amount of capital devoted to their employment	Wages depend on the margin of cultivation, falling as it falls and rising as it rises
Interest depends upon the supply and demand for capital; or as is stated of profits, upon wages (or the cost of labor), rising as wages fall, and falling as wages rise	Interest (its ratio with wages being fixed by the net power of increase which attaches to capital), depends on the margin of cultivation, falling as it falls and rising as it rises

As George put the comparisons:

"In the current statement the laws of distribution have no common center, no mutual relation; they are not the correlating divisions of a whole, but measures of different qualities. In the statement we have given, they spring from one point, support and supplement each other, and form the correlating divisions of a complete whole."

George now summarized his intellectual achievements as having provided a clear, simple, and consistent theory of the distribution of wealth which accords with first principles and existing facts, and which, when fully understood, is self-evident.

He continued his summarization as follows:

"Nothing can be clearer than the proposition that the failure of wages to increase (proportionately) with increasing productive power is due to the increase of rent.

"Three things unite to production—labor, capital, and land. Three parties divide the produce—the laborer, the capitalist, and the landowner. If, with an increase of production the laborer gets no more and the capitalist gets no more, it is a necessary inference that the landowner reaps the whole gain."

The complexities of production in the civilized state, where exchange plays so large a role in production, and so much labor is applied to materials after they have been separated from land, should not obscure the essential truth that all production is still the union of the three factors, land, labor, and capital, and that rent cannot be increased except at the expense of wages and interest.

He concluded his summary of the unity of the laws of production he established with such great intellectual effort with the following politically economic statement:

"It is the general fact, observable everywhere, that as the value of land increases, so does the contrast between wealth and want appear. It is the universal fact that, where the value of land is highest, civilization exhibits the greatest luxury side by side with the most piteous destitution."

12

A DEMURRAL

As he indicated that he might in his introduction to this work, the author has determined to demur at this time from a basic assumption made by Henry George, because the author perceives that the insightful reader, from the perspective of the twenty-first century, is likely to do so himself or herself.

Commencing with his demolition of the "wages fund" theory, through the development of the laws of rent, wages, and interest, and their coordination, George has consistently placed labor and capital on the progressive side of the equation: Produce—rent = wages + interest.

With hindsight, it is almost impossible to accept the view that capital and labor at the time of publication of Progress and Poverty in 1879, were equal sufferers at the hands of land. The weak and ineffectual claims of labor, even before 1879, could hardly be compared to the vigorous and almost irresistible thrust and claims of capital. In the last quarter of the nineteenth century, following the impetus provided by the Civil War, the "Robber Barons" were riding high and roughshod over labor.

Why George was virtually blind to this disparity, and persisted in viewing capital as on a par, and no more, with labor, can only be speculated upon.

The first thought which comes to the author's mind is that, so focused was George on the political economic model drawn from an agricultural society, which he was determined to overturn, that even while having expanded his definition of land to include all the planet's "natural endowments," his laws of rent, wages, and interest depended fundamentally upon the agricultural model.

The irony of the situation is (as has previously been hinted at by the author) that having turned a blind eye to what would develop through the following century into full-fledged, imperious capitalism, George's insights into the predatory and dominant position of the owners of land (as mineral resources, particularly fuel) in feeding the world's giant industrial systems, would prove to be prescient and correct.

Nevertheless, before proceeding with a continuing summary of George's analysis and arguments, which are cogent and relevant, save for the equal statuses of wages and interest—the returns to labor and capital respectively—the author feels it necessary to present an analysis of George's political economy in which capital and labor are shown not to be in harmonious opposition to rent, but in conflict.

This conceptual presentation, if convincing, is certainly in accord with real world experience for well over a century.

Among the earliest industrial-type enterprises in Western Europe undoubtedly was the grist mill, where farmers brought their grain harvest for milling into flour. Such a mill required placement along a stream with sufficiently steady flow, adequate power, and a low incidence of flooding. Also, the stream's banks had to be firm and stable enough to support the structure housing the milling, bagging, and storing functions.

Whether in feudal times or the latter period of individual rights in the product of one's own labor, the erection of a mill required considerable capital. Such capital in feudal times would in all likelihood rest in the possession of the local lord, who almost certainly owned the land upon which a grist mill would be erected.

It is just possible that a tradesman from a nearby chartered town, perhaps a successful carpenter/builder, might approach the local lord with the offer to purchase from him a parcel of land on the stream just large enough to erect a grist mill with accompanying right of access.

Let us suppose that the lord, whose earned rent for his land consisted of a large part of the produce, had been required to have his grain milled some distance away. Since a grist mill on or adjacent to his land would certainly add value to his produce, he looked somewhat favorably upon the project, and countered the builder's offer to buy with an offer to lease land upon which a mill might be erected.

The builder, aware that renting land would subject his mill and its produce to the virtually capricious exactions to which the lord's tenant farmers were subject, politely declined the offer to lease the land.

The lord, sensing the earnings potential of the mill, cleverly offered to enter into a partnership with the builder, a partnership covering both land and mill.

The builder, just as cleverly, sensed the probability of a conflict of interest on the lord's part, where the lord might utilize his leverage as a large customer, even though a partner, to pressure the builder.

Finally, considering the benefit of a proximate mill, the lord agreed to sell some land; the remaining question being that of establishing a mutually satisfactory price for the land.

As there existed a prevailing value (or price) for local farm land, that was the opening bid on the part of the builder. The lord initially rejected such price as representing no real gain over the existing farming tenancy.

The builder spoke of the loss of present income on his capital in the course of its conversion to a mill, as well as the risk of greater loss should the venture prove less profitable than hoped for.

He then made the following proposal: that since, he, the builder, could fairly accurately estimate the cost of the erected mill, and the value of the land was established by the existing market, then the enterprise be capitalized on that proportionate basis with other local known possessors of capital invited in to share ownership proportionately. All risks and benefits would be shared; and as wages for laborers would be the same as at the agricultural margin of productivity, capacity known, and prices of grinding fairly accurately estimated, a return in excess of farming or capital otherwise employed in town or loaned out, was calculated. An agreement was executed on that basis, and the hegemony of land was thusly broken by a capitalistic enterprise which could, on a given parcel of land, with the application of substantial capital, yield far in excess of produce or wealth per acre than could be obtained by the most intensive agricultural production.

Resorting to our favorite equation:

Produce—Rent = Wages + Interest

If rent (or its capitalized value) approaches zero, and the increasing produce is shared by labor and capital, where the law of wages continues to prevail as for agricultural land, surely the return in interest to capital must increase.

How then, through capitalist development, could labor and capital prosper equally?

Capital has another extraordinary quality not shared by land or labor, of which it is compounded. Land, for all practical purposes is finite; it cannot be produced. The capacity of labor through the working life of a laborer, is also finite. But capital can, and does aggregate from generation to generation, despite amortization, in perpetuity.

So abundant is capital at present that trillions of dollars each day slosh freely around the planet in search of investment or speculative opportunities. Whole regional economies are impacted by such developmental inflows, and as quickly devastated by equally rapid outflow to seemingly more promising venues. Capital is surely a case of the child outgrowing and overshadowing its parent—until, as will be shown, it is itself overshadowed.

The fictional example previously presented was intended to show a likely first step in the beginnings of Capitalism. It was not designed to demonstrate the diminished import of land in production, since no production is possible without land in all its forms; but was intended to illustrate superior productivity of

41

land by the application of labor, aided by the harnessing of energy through relatively simple technology.

Inasmuch as relatively small parcels of land, often agriculturally unproductive land, could be obtained, which would support relatively highly productive enterprises without being subject to the law of rent, such enterprises were extremely attractive to owners of capital seeking investment opportunities.

The subsequent march of capitalism to its present form is a great story unto itself, and has been introduced here only in an effort to amend what the author perceived as either a deliberate omission on the part of Henry George as an irrelevant factor in the increase of poverty with the concurrent increase of overall community wealth, or a genuine belief that interest and wages were inherently linked by a mechanism causing the maintenance of equilibrium.

In pursuing an understanding of the relevance of George's political economy, with its focus on the pivotal role of land in the distribution of produce, it is necessary to remember the concurrent development of capitalism to its predominant position in the twentieth century.

A resumed study of George's thesis will demonstrate its continuing relevance as capital grew to a position of dominance over labor.

13

THE EFFECTS OF MATERIAL
PROGRESS ON DISTRIBUTION

Having established to his satisfaction that rent is the receiver of
the increased production that material progress provides, Henry
George asked the question: what is the force or necessity that,
as productive power increases, distributes a greater and greater
proportion of the product as rent?

"The only cause pointed out by Ricardo as advancing rent is
the increase of population, which by requiring larger supplies of
food, necessitates the extension of cultivation to inferior lands, or
to points of inferior production on the same land," wrote George.

George agreed that the increasing pressure of population
compels a resort to inferior points of production, which will raise
rents, and does in fact raise rents (as previously described), but
asserted strongly that there are other causes. In order to establish
what these other causes are, and how they operate, he undertook
to trace the effect of material progress upon the distribution of
wealth.

George then listed the three changes which contribute to
material progress: (1) increase in population; (2) improvements in

the arts of production and exchange; (3) improvement in knowledge, education, government, police, manners and morals, so far as they increase the power of producing wealth.

To better ascertain the effects of material progress upon wealth distribution, he proposed to consider the effects of increased population without reference to improvement in the arts, and then the effects of improvement in the arts apart from increase of population.

As considered in the light of material forces or economies, the increase in knowledge, the betterment of government, etc., have the same effect as improvement in the arts: George therefore believed that it would not be necessary to consider them separately.

The manner in which increasing population advances rent is explained by the increased demand for subsistence, which forces production to inferior productive points. If, with a given population, the margin of cultivation is at 30, all lands of productive power over 30 will pay rent. If the population is doubled, and additional supply is required, which cannot be obtained without an extension of cultivation, that will cause lands to yield rent that before yielded none. If the extension is to 20, then all lands between 20 and 30 will yield rent and have value, and all land over 30 will yield increased rent and have increased value.

It is here that the Malthusian doctrine secures support from the theory of rent. According to John Stuart Mill, although two hands come into the world with each mouth, it becomes harder and harder for the new hands to supply the new mouth.

As described by Ricardo and those economists who have followed him, the advance in rents which experience shows accompany increasing population is caused by the inability to procure more food except at greater cost, which forces the margin of production to lower and lower points of production, commensurately increasing rent.

A clarification appears to be called for here, since the "greater cost" at the margin does not comport with the Georgian rendition of the law of rent, as follows: "The rent of land is determined by the excess of its produce over that which THE SAME APPLICATION

OF LABOR (emphasis by the author) can secure from the least productive land in use."

It is the "same application" at the margin yielding lesser production, which has the effect of increasing overall prices, thereby achieving the same result as that of increasing rent.

George then stressed that he wished to reject the presumption that the recourse to a lower point of production necessarily involved a smaller aggregate product in proportion to the labor expended, for increased population of itself, without any advance in the arts, implied an increase in the productive power of labor. The labor of 100 men, other things being equal, will produce much more that 100 times the labor of one man, and the labor of 1,000 men much more than ten times the labor of 100 men. And so, with every additional pair of hands which increasing population brings, there is more than a proportionate addition to the productive power of labor.

Consequently, with increasing population, there may be recourse to lower power of production, not only with diminution in the average production of wealth as compared to labor, but without any diminution at the lowest point. The increased effectiveness of labor which comes by reason of increased population that compels resort to the inferior quality of land attaches to all labor, and the gain on the superior qualities of land will more than compensate for the diminished production on the quality last brought in. The aggregate wealth production, as compared with the aggregate expenditure of labor will be great, though its distribution will be more unequal.

Thus, increase of population, as it operates to extend production to lower levels, operates to increase rent and reduce wages as a proportion, and may, or may not, reduce wages as a quantity; while it seldom can, and probably never does, reduce the aggregate production of wealth as compared to the aggregate expenditure of labor, but on the contrary increases, and frequently largely increases it. The increased powers of cooperation and exchanges which come with increased population are equivalent to and provide increased capacity to land.

The beginnings of sparsely populated settlements and their subsequent growth into villages, towns and cities is always accompanied by multiplying aggregate wealth, increased rent on land, and a proportionate diminution of the return to labor and capital, which proportion, in absolute terms may, or may not, increase with growth. This will occur even during periods of negligible advance in the arts and technology, simply by virtue of proximate cooperation and exchange.

14

EFFECTS OF IMPROVEMENT IN THE ARTS

Now, having eliminated from examination the effects of increasing population upon the distribution of wealth, Henry George proceeded to analyze the effects of improvement in the arts.

George now boldly asserted, "We have seen that increase of population increases rent, rather by increasing the productiveness of labor than by decreasing it. It can now be shown that, irrespective of the increase in population, the effect of improvement in methods of production and exchange is to increase rent, the disproof of the Malthusian theory—and of all the doctrines derived from or related to it—will be final and complete, for we will have accounted for the tendency of material progress to lower wages and depress the condition of the lowest class, without recourse to the theory of increasing pressure against the means of subsistence."

George mused that if the existing power of labor were capable of satisfying all material desire, with no possibility of new desire being called forth, the effect of labor saving devices would be simply to reduce the amount of labor expended.

However, inasmuch as human desire for material things appears virtually infinitely expansible, the amount of wealth produced is nowhere commensurate with the desire for wealth, and desire increases with every additional opportunity for gratification. This being the case, the effect of labor saving improvements is to increase the production of wealth. Now, for the production of wealth two things are required—labor and land. Therefore the effect of labor saving improvements is to extend the demand for land for application by the, in effect, expanded labor supply, and to bring into cultivation lands of less natural productiveness. So, while the primary effect of labor saving improvements is to increase the power of labor, the secondary effect is to extend cultivation and, where this lowers the margin of cultivation, to increase rent.

Consequently, the ultimate effect of labor saving machinery or improvements is to increase rent without increasing wages or interest proportionately.

George insisted that this be fully understood, since it shows that effects attributed to increase of population are really due to the progress of invention and explained the otherwise perplexing fact that labor saving machinery everywhere failed to benefit laborers.

It must be remembered that when George wrote of labor or laborers, he meant those who engage in human exertion of any and all kinds in producing wealth or engaging in exchange, in contrast to land or capital, in generic terms.

George went to great lengths to demonstrate the interchangeability of wealth, and wrote, "I am unable to think of any form of wealth, the demand for which would not be increased by a saving in the labor required to produce the others." And every increase in the power of producing any form of wealth must result in an increased demand for land and the direct products of land.

Concisely stated, George wrote: "Wealth in all its forms, being the product of labor applied to land or the products of land, any increase in the power of labor, the demand for wealth being unsatisfied, will be used in procuring more wealth, and thus increase the demand for land."

To further illustrate the capacity of improvement in the arts to produce precisely those effects attributed to increase of population, George imagined a country where land is in possession of a portion of the people and a permanent barrier is fixed to further increase in population by enforcement of a Herodian law.

He arbitrarily set the margin of cultivation, or production at 20. Thus, land or other natural opportunities which, from the application of labor and capital, will yield a return of 20, will just give the ordinary rate of wages and interest, without yielding any rent; while all lands yielding to equal applications of labor and capital more than 20 will yield the excess as rent. Population remaining fixed, let there be made inventions and improvements which will reduce by one-tenth the expenditure of labor and capital necessary to produce the same amount of wealth. Now, either one-tenth the labor and capital may be freed, and production remain the same as before; or the same amount of capital and labor be employed and production correspondingly increased. Owing to the increased efficiency of labor (uncompensated) secured by the new improvements, as great a return can be secured at the point of natural productivity represented by 18, as before at 20. The rent would be increased by the difference between 18 and 20, while wages and interest in quantity, would be no more than before, and in proportion to the whole process would be less. There would be greater production of wealth, but landowners would get the whole benefit.

If invention and improvement continue, the efficiency of labor will further increase and the amount of labor and capital necessary to achieve a given result (per unit of production) will diminish. The same causes will lead to the utilization of this new gain in productive power for production of more wealth; the margin of cultivation will again be extended and rent will rise, both in proportion and amount, without any increase in wages and interest. And so, as invention and improvement go on, adding to the efficiency of labor, the margin of production will be pushed lower and lower, and rent constantly increased, though population should remain stationary.

George wished to make clear that it was not precisely true that labor set free by each improvement will all be driven to seek employment in production of more wealth.

"The increased power of satisfaction which each improvement gives to a certain portion of the community will be utilized in demanding leisure or services, as well as demanding wealth. Some laborers will therefore, become idlers and some will pass from the ranks of productive to those of unproductive laborers—a proportion of which, as observation shows, tends to increase with the progress of society.

"All that I wish to make clear is that, without any increase in population, the progress of invention constantly tends to give a larger proportion of the produce to the owners of land, and a smaller and smaller proportion to labor and capital."

The point of absolute perfection of labor saving inventions may seem remote, if not impossible of attainment; but it is a point toward which the march of invention is every day more strongly tending, particularly in our era of artificial intelligence and digital communication and control.

The author will subsequently direct his attention to this matter in the context of the efflorescence and metamorphosis of Capitalism from its bourgeois beginnings.

In the improvements which advance rents are not only to be included the improvements which directly increase productive power, but also such improvements in government, manners, and morals as indirectly increase it by enhancing the ease and efficiency of cooperative behavior and exchange within the community.

15

"LAND" EQUATES TO NATURAL RESOURCES

As the author of this work intends to expand upon the significance of "margin of cultivation" or "margin of production" as regards their application to national and international manufacturing and commerce, he feels it necessary to expound upon the terms, graphically and verbally

As has been stated before, the term "land" is interchangeable with "natural resource," although in virtually all of George's analyses, the images conjured up appear to refer to the earth's surface as utilized for agriculture. This is undoubtedly due to the original theoretical basis for defining and justifying rent being rooted in an era when large landed estates were held and rented out in parcels by barons and noblemen who had frequently received those land grants from the king, the ultimate owner of all "real" (royal) estate. The land, as agricultural resource, for eons, was in effect the source of virtually all wealth, and it was understandable that efforts to justify rent upon land would essentially confine itself to agricultural land.

Below is an illustration portraying land in reasonable proximity and differing productivity intended to demonstrate the "margin of cultivation."

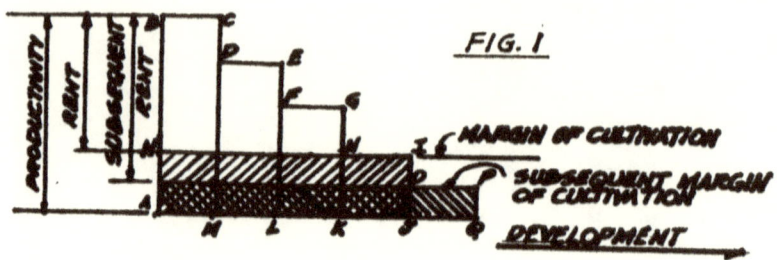

FIG. 1

The rectangle HIJK represents either the productivity of "free land" or that of land of the lowest relative productivity in a geographic area in private ownership where the quantities of labor and capital utilized for each rectangle (per acre) are equal. The line NHI represents the boundary which defines the line above which rent is considered justified, as signifying the relative greater value of the land. In short, the tenant of each parcel of differing productivity is obliged to yield to the owner of his parcel rent in the amount above the margin of cultivation. So, as far as the tenant is concerned, it does not matter what the productivity of his rented land is, as the income remaining to him after paying rent is the same as if he were farming the least productive land HIJK.

The phenomenon described above is primarily due to the fact that wages (the return to labor) is maintained as uniform by the owners of land, and where circumstances of any kind, such as described by Henry George, force an extension to land of reduced productivity, OPQJ, the percentage of produce or product taken by rent increases as a proportion of productivity, even though the absolute quantity remaining to labor and capital, may, or may not, increase by virtue of accompanying increased overall productivity.

It must be understood that labor had only the choice of accepting those terms, emigrating, or starving.

By way of illustration, a contemporary commercial example will be portrayed.

A young man works as a clerk in a retail store in the center of a regional city, to which he commutes daily from his recently acquired home in the suburbs, as he cannot afford to live close to his work, where rents are high.

He has, over time, achieved a high degree of proficiency in his work, but increasingly finds the expense and wear and tear on both himself and his automobile onerous, and finally decides to explore the possibility and practicality of opening a retail shop of the same type in his young, outlying district.

Having some knowledge of the rent his employer pays in the city, and much knowledge of the high volume of traffic on the adjacent streets, he inquires as to the rents of available suitable sites in his suburb, while observing the much smaller volume of foot traffic on the adjacent streets.

Based upon his experience in the city, he seeks an available location near a source of community activity, namely a store on the same block as the one movie house in town.

The rent asked is reasonable by city standards, and with funds borrowed from his and his wife' relatives, as well as virtually all his savings, he signs a lease with the property owner. The lease stipulates, among many terms clearly to the property owner's advantage, the monthly rent of an escalating annual rent clause for the ten years of the lease.

The young entrepreneur, with the assistance of a store designer, sets out to furnish the store attractively and, based upon his experience in his line of work, receives limited credit from suppliers with whom he has dealt.

Unbeknownst to the young businessman, his suburb and others surrounding the city represent the "margin of cultivation" or "margin of productivity" of the region, barring the agricultural land beyond the suburbs. The closer to the city, the higher are rents, the portion of productivity taken by the owners of land and improvements. In the city itself, rents as well as the volume of exchange are the highest of the region, entirely due to the highest density of population.

The volume of business the young man experiences is much lower than he was accustomed to, and he must maintain prices calibrated just high enough to discourage residents of his suburb from shopping in the city. In time he builds up a clientele and manages to derive a living from his enterprise, a living barely high enough to pay off his relatives and recoup some of his savings. He congratulates himself on not only surviving, but for being able to live in a fairly uncrowded community with a good school for his children. His wife, in order to help in refunding loans to relatives, has taken a "temporary" job in the city, as wages for women in the suburbs would be lower, as opportunities are fewer.

Fortunately for our entrepreneur, the region experiences growth, and new suburbs further from the city are developed, a few containing industrial parks.

In consequence of the region's growth, business in our young businessman's shop increases and, despite the increased rent he is obliged to pay as the years pass, he does reasonably well.

The margin of productivity has now passed to the new further suburbs, and the now maturing businessman is paying more rent each year, as contracted in his lease. He has seen, and profited from the increased development in his suburb, now a town, but he begins to worry as to what will occur when his lease is up within three years.

He is advised to speak to his landlord, with whom he has maintained good relations over the years well before his lease is due to expire. He seeks to do so, but is informed that his landlord is on a cruise around the world for three months. He can scarcely wait for his return.

Upon his landlord's return, he casually broaches the matter of lease renewal with him and is politely informed that, with growth of the town, there is an increasing demand for space, and that it is premature to speak of a lease renewal. The landlord politely remarks that he might even demolish our entrepreneurs building, along with the four others alongside it to accommodate a large national chain of merchants.

This is one of many possible examples of the operation of the phenomenon of the "margin of cultivation" or "margin of productivity."

A somewhat different scenario involves a small manufacturing plant in the general vicinity of our entrepreneur's building. The firm is still family owned, having been established a generation before the present owner/manager's control. The factory building, including accessory offices, is situated on considerable acreage, the land having been bought from the estate of a retiring farmer at reasonable cost, in light of current suburban values. Most of the land is used for parking, loading and unloading, and for temporary outdoor storage.

Regional prosperity, with increased population in city and suburbs, has had not only a modest impact upon the business, which sells to a multi-state customer base; however, the pool of potential employees has grown, permitting an improvement in employee quality.

With the passage of years, as in the case of our first entrepreneur, the growth of the suburb into a town has surrounded the manufacturing plant with some family homes and a couple of small malls. A change in zoning would not permit such a plant in its present location today, but the property is "grandfathered in," and may be legally continued in its present use, but not expanded.

The owner of the plant has now been approached by real estate brokers representing developers, who have offered a premium price for the land. The owner of the facility rejects all offers, as he wishes to leave the business intact to a third generation of the same family.

Eventually, a seasoned broker offers the owner the following proposition:

1. A price for his property, the income from which, at current interest rates, would approximate his income from the factory; or put another way, would capitalize at the present value of his business.

2. A parcel of undeveloped land of the same acreage several miles out in the hinterland with equivalent road and rail

access.

3. Payment for access to equivalent utilities on the new property enjoyed at the existing plant.

The plant owner considers the offer in light of the potential benefits of: the means to build and equip a more modern plant not too distant from present employees and suppliers, the opportunity to expand the new plant at will, a more bucolic and serene environment devoid of traffic congestion and complaining townspeople, an avoidance of possible, rumored confiscation by eminent domain of his property for a new high school

He accepts the offer as, unwittingly, the beneficiary of the extension and lowering of the "margin of cultivation" or "margin of production" beyond his property, in a direction away from the largest, most viable large town or city.

Although the owner of his land, its value can be translated into a capital possession costing a virtual rent loss of an annual series of equivalence at prevailing interest rates in perpetuity.

As owner, his rental payment to himself has been increased by the extension of the margins of "cultivation" or "production."

These two illustrations show the presumptive present day operation of the law of rent promulgated well over 250 years ago, and manifested much earlier with the private ownership of land.

In earlier times, where lands were held in joint communal or tribal ownership, the fact of variable qualities of land was dealt with by a system of temporary rotational cultivation by families of the community or tribe. Among the American Indians, as well as other peoples still retaining roots in a hunting and fish era, the concept of privately owned land was considered incredible and barbaric. Although tribes might make war over access to land and its fruits, such hostilities were always conducted for shared tribal benefits in land.

16

DEVIATING FROM THE LAW OF RENT

A review of the previous chapter, in which the author has attempted to illustrate the operation of the "Law of Rent" under contemporary circumstances with two examples, following a graphic example of the "Law of Rent," has brought to the fore a disjunction between the two examples and the law as described and illustrated.

The "Law of Rent" stipulates that "the same application of labor and capital" be applied to each parcel of varying productivity, and therefore each parcel return an equal amount as wages and interest, leaving the rest as rent. However, the conceptual construction can be approximated in reality only under feudal control of wages and mobility.

Both examples offered, in order to approximate actual modern circumstances, indicate that, not only is productivity higher in the city than the suburbs, but wages—the return to labor are also higher.

We know that this in fact is so. The highest populated areas, where infrastructure and technology are likely to be the most highly developed, do return the highest wages, contrary to the classical "law of rent" or the "law of wages."

What is likely to account for this discrepancy?

Perhaps we have to begin with the capacity of a large population, as George described it, to enhance productivity above and beyond its tendency to cause a reduction in the margin of cultivation. The effect of improvements in the arts, most likely to occur within large population centers, acts to produce a similar enhancement of productivity as do improvements in education, government, and all civilizing influences.

However, all of these enhancements in productivity are compatible only with a great division of labor and the creation of a complex hierarchy of skills. These developments cannot occur without providing for higher wages for more demanding skills and more onerous types of work. By definition, the classical model of undifferentiated labor and wages is incapable of encompassing the capitalist industrial model.

George should surely have been aware of the significant real world shift from the classical Ricardo model of rent by observing the wide range of wages currently being paid for work requiring different skills. Extant trade unions fought vigorously to secure suitable wages for skilled craftsmen and artisans. It is almost as if George refused, or was unable, to clearly see in the rapid rise of the capitalist class, the decoupling of his cherished view of labor and capital equally abused and exploited by the owners of land. His vision thusly obscured, he was in no position to see the need for modification and upgrading of the classic "law of rent."

The classic laws of rent and wages were, in effect, snapshots in fixed time of a static system; and unsuited to capture or describe accurately a rapidly changing era where capital was becoming master of the spirally expanding industrial movement.

Is there a possibility of reconciling the discrepancy between a classical "law of rent," based on the seminal work of Ricardo, with contemporary political economic reality? Yes!

If the diagram previously presented displaying the function of the margin of cultivation is amended to incorporate George's three changes which contribute to material progress, namely:

(1) Increase in population

(2) Improvement in the arts of production and exchange

(3) Improvement in knowledge, education, government, etc., etc.— then the political economic reality of yesterday, today, and tomorrow can be diagrammatically portrayed as follows:

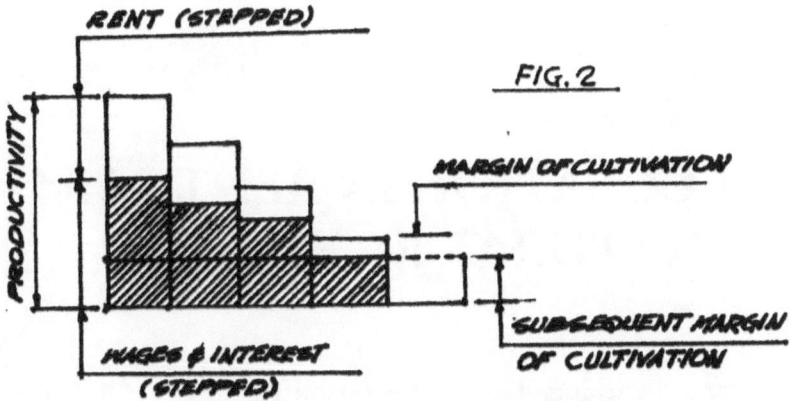

17

SPECULATION IN RENTS AND NATURAL RESOURCES

George now introduced the expectation of future enhancement of land values into his analysis of the distribution of wealth in consequence of material progress.

There was in all progressive countries the confident expectation that a steady increase of rent would cause a continuing rise in land values, thereby encouraging land speculation.

It had been assumed in studying the operation of the law of rent that the actual margin of cultivation would always coincide with what George termed the necessary margin of cultivation—that was to say that cultivation extended to less productive points only as it became necessary from the fact that natural opportunities were at the more productive points fully utilized. "This probably is the case in stationary or very slowly progressing communities, but in rapidly progressing communities, where the swift and steady increase of rent gives confidence to calculations of further increase, it is not the case.

"In such communities, the confident expectation of increased prices produces, to a greater or lesser extent, the effects of a combination among land holders, and tends to the withholding of land from use in expectation of higher prices, thus forcing the margin of cultivation farther than required by the necessities of production," wrote George.

In countries where the tenant system of agriculture is weak, this cause operates more in the selling price of land, rather than in rent.

"This phenomenon may still be observed in every rapidly growing city, where empty lots utilized as parking fields (which thrive while awaiting the suitable time for development precisely because of the great human and vehicular population) await the suitable time for building.

"But when the limits of the growing city are reached, the actual margin of building, which corresponds to the margin of cultivation in agriculture—it is found that the land is not purchasable at its value for agricultural purposes, as it would be were rent determined by present day requirements; but for a long distance beyond the city, land bears a speculative value.

"It is well known that there are individuals described as 'land poor'—that is, who remain poor, sometimes almost to deprivation, because they insist on holding land, which they themselves cannot use, at prices at which no one else can profitably use it."

To illustrate how land speculation may ensure that rent will increase in greater proportion than the increase of productive power, George offered the following example:

"With the margin of cultivation standing at 20, an increase in the power of production takes place which renders the same result obtainable with one-tenth less labor. For reasons before stated, the margin of production must now be forced down, and if it rests at 18, the return to labor and capital will be the same as before, when the margin stood at 20. Whether it will be forced to 18, or be forced lower, depends on what I have called the area of productiveness, which intervenes between 20 and 18. But if the confident expectation of further increase in rents lead the landowner to demand 3 rent for 20 land, 2 for 19, and 1 for 18 land, and to withhold his land from use until these terms are complied with, the area of productiveness may be so reduced that the margin of cultivation must fall to 17 or even lower; and thus, as the result of the increase in efficiency of labor, laborers would get less than before, while interest would <u>be proportionately reduced, and rent would increase in greater ratio than the increase in productive power."</u>

Here we have presented a most challenging proposition, demanding particular scrutiny, especially in light of the following conclusions he draws on the subject of land speculation—which, it must be remembered—is speculation in all of the earth's natural endowments.

"The cause which limits speculation in commodities, the tendency of increasing price to draw forth additional supplies, cannot limit the speculative advance in land values, as land is a fixed quantity, which human agency can neither increase nor diminish; but there is never the less a limit to the price of land in the minimum required by labor and capital as the condition of engaging in production..."

Now, it is not entirely true that land is a fixed quantity, as has been shown by numerous examples where marginal or semi-desert areas have been made fruitful by irrigation and new techniques for controlled application of limited water resources. Terracing of utterly unsuited mountainous areas for stepped agricultural production has been utilized for centuries; and a dramatic increase in oil prices by the Organization of Petroleum Exporting Countries (OPEC) invariably sets off an energetic and frequently successful search for new petroleum resources.

However, for theoretical and most practical purposes the assumption of a limited supply of land is, at present, and certainly in the near future, a reasonable operating assumption.

18

TRANSITIONING FROM "LAND" TO NATURAL RESOURCES

George now advanced his theory of the causes of industrial depressions, for which he primarily blamed periodic speculative expansions. These periodic paroxysms he held to be but aggravated examples of normal phenomena constantly tending to lower the margin of production, thereby reducing returns to labor and capital and decreasing demand.

Although George, in the earlier part of *PROGRESS AND POVERTY* emphasized that "land" and "natural resources" (all natural endowments) are equivalent, he continued to employ the term "land" even when very likely done for the simplicity of the single word "land" and possibly for reasons of continuity or habit.

"Rent," or the return to "land," where the natural resource is not agricultural, but mineral (or otherwise), is not a fixed periodic payment, but outright payment for purchases, thereby expanding and altering somewhat the meaning of "rent" for George.

Now, it will be recalled that under some conditions, and in some communities of high productivity, even though rent will sweep away a larger proportion of product, paradoxically, the absolute return to labor and capital may be increasing, accounting for "good times" with increasing demand even as the margin of productivity declines.

This phenomenon will be intensified and hastened (as shown in the prior chapter) when speculation is at a high pitch. In point of fact, every depression, or recession has been preceded by a feverish expansion, and heralded by a sudden, sharp faltering of real estate values and general construction.

The ensuing depression demonstrates itself by the accumulation of unsold inventory, which imposes a curtailment of production from industry to industry as those workers laid off in one plant or industry are unable to purchase the product of others.

According to George, "The period of depression thus ensuing would continue until (1) The speculative advance in rents has been lost; or (2) the increase in the efficiency of labor, owing to the growth of population and the progress of improvement, had enabled the normal rent line to overtake the speculative rent line; or (3) labor and capital had reconciled to engaging in production for smaller returns. Or, most probably, all three of these causes would cooperate to produce a new equilibrium, at which point all forces of production would again engage, and a season of activity ensue; whereupon rent would begin to advance again, a speculative advance again takes place, production again be checked, and the same round be gone over."

Previously, George has shown that a period of exuberant speculation causes an expansion of the need for land, causing the margin of production to drop excessively, thereby increasing rent and proportionately diminishing interest and wages. If this speculative advance should be accompanied by a burst of technical or societal enhancement of productivity, the absolute return to labor and capital may keep pace or even exceed the preceding returns. But, as there is no organic connection between the two phenomena, the speculative advance reaching a point of market saturation quite independently, the margin of production must, in time, return to the "normal" rent line, with diminished returns to labor and capital.

The author will expand upon the phenomenon of periodic productivity dysfunctionality subsequently, as he carries the Georgian methodology into the advanced capitalist production.

George commented caustically upon the contending explanations for periodic depressions by contemporaneous schools of opinion. One school had it that speculation produced depressions by causing overproduction, another opined that over-consumption was the culprit, having made consumers extravagant by fictitious prosperity and causing them to live unsustainably beyond their means.

George regarded each of the two explanations as expressing one side or phase of a general truth, with each one failing to comprehend the full truth.

"As an explanation of the phenomena, each is equally and utterly preposterous," observed George. "For while the great masses of men want more wealth than they can get, and while they are willing to give for it that which is the basis and raw material of wealth—their labor—how can there be overproduction? And while the machinery of production wastes, and producers are condemned to unwilling idleness, how can there be over consumption?

"Clearly, the trouble is that production and consumption cannot meet and satisfy each other because of the speculation in land, as demonstrated previously." George goes on to proclaim that in each period of high industrial activity, land values have risen steadily, culminating in speculation, followed by a partial cessation of production and its corollary, cessation of effective demand, generally followed by a commercial crash.

He proceeded to amplify his thesis, as follows:

"All trade, let it be remembered, is the exchange of commodities for commodities, and hence the cessation of demand for some commodities, which marks the depression of trade, is really a cessation in the supply of other commodities.

"In common parlance we say that 'buyers have no money,' or that 'money is becoming scarce,' but in talking this way we ignore the fact that money is but a medium of exchange. What buyers lack is not money, but commodities which they can turn into money—what is really becoming scarce is product of some sort.

The diminution of the effective demand of consumers is therefore but a result of the diminishing of production."

George now asserted that the industrial pyramid manifestly rests on land. The primary and fundamental occupations, which create a demand for all others, are evidently those which extract wealth from nature, and therefore, if we trace from one exchange point to another, the check on production, which shows itself in decreased purchasing power, we ultimately find it in some obstacle which checks labor in expending itself on land. And that obstacle, it is clear, is the speculative advance in land, or the value of land, which produces the same effects as a lockout of labor and capital by landowners.

Again, the reader is reminded that "land," as the term is used by George, and in this work, is "all natural endowments," not simply agricultural, commercial, or industrial land. Mineral deposits, great fishing banks, great cataracts capable of generating power, etc. all fall under this heading.

The perceptive reader will surely observe that what George found to be true as regards depressions (now called recessions) is as plausible today as it was in 1879!

Clearly, if those made unemployed during depressions were producing wealth from the land, they would not only be employing themselves, but would be employing others—mechanics, store keepers, actors and musicians, and workers in other trades and industries through the demand they would be creating.

What prevents labor from employing itself on land? Simply that land has been monopolized and is frequently held at speculative prices, based not upon the present value, but upon the added value that will come with the future growth of population and demand.

"Each form of industry, as it is developed by division of labor, springs from and rises out of the others, and all rest ultimately on land; for without land, labor is as impotent as would be a man in void space. To make the illustration closer to the condition of a progressive country, imagine a pyramid composed of superimposed layers—the whole constantly growing and expanding. Imagine the growth of the layer nearest the ground to be checked. The others will for a time keep on expanding—in fact, for the moment the tendency will be to quicker expansion, for the vital force which is refused scope on the ground layer will strive to vent in those—until at length, there is a decided overbalance and a sudden crumbling along all the faces of the pyramid," observed George.

"A depression then runs its course, in the manner previously described, and a new equilibrium is then established, which will result in another season of comparative activity. The normal rent line and the speculative rent line are brought together (1) by the customary fall in speculative land values, which is very evident in the reduction of rents and shrinkage of real estate values in the principal cities, (2) by the increased efficiency of labor, arising from the growth of population and the utilization of new inventions and discoveries, (3) by the lowering of the habitual standard of interest and wages. Which as to interest, is shown by the progressive general decline of interest rates during the most recent recession."

19

THE PERSISTENT DECLINE OF LABOR'S SHARE OF PRODUCTION

Henry George now proceeded to observe that the decline of wages could only be persistent, however great the productive power of labor, because of the constant aggregation of an increasing share of production to rent. While he allowed that even with a decreasing percentage of productive value tending to labor representing, on occasion, an increase in absolute terms, the general trend had to be a decline of labor's share of produced wealth.

He then proceeded to a sociological analysis of the portent to labor of those activities which accompany an increase of productive power in a progressive community, which, without the benefits a continuous increase in labor's share of production, tends to reduce the free laborer to the helpless and degraded condition of a slave.

George wrote, "All improvements which add to productive power as civilization advances consist in, or necessitate, a still further sub-division of labor, and the efficiency of the whole body of laborers is increased at the expense of the independence of the constituents. The individual laborer acquires knowledge of and skill in but an infinitesimal part of the varied processes which are required to supply even the commonest wants. The aggregate produce of the labor of a savage tribe is small, but each member is capable of an independent life...

"The simple theory which I have outlined (if indeed it can be called a theory, which is but the recognition of the most obvious relations) explains the conjunction of poverty with wealth, of low wages with high productive power, of degradation with enlightenment, of virtual slavery in political liberty.

"In all our long investigation we have been advancing to this simplistic truth: that land is necessary to the exertion of labor in the production of wealth, to command the land which is necessary to labor is to command all the fruits of labor save enough to enable labor to exist. We have been advancing as through an enemy's country, in which every step must be secured, every position fortified, and every by-path explored; for this simple truth, in its application to social and political problems is hidden from the masses of men partly by its very simplicity, and in greater part by widespread fallacies and erroneous habits of thought which lead them to look in every direction but the right one for an explanation of the evils which oppress and threaten the civilized world...

"The great cause of inequality in the distribution of wealth is inequality in the ownership of land. The ownership of land is the great fundamental fact which ultimately determines the social, the political, and consequently the intellectual and moral condition of people...

"Everywhere, and in all times, among all peoples, the possession of land is the base of aristocracy, the foundation of great fortunes, the source of power."

These assertions will subsequently be examined in light of the preponderant growth of capital in relation to labor, as Capitalism itself grew to become the dominant factor in a spreading global economic system.

20

COMMONLY PROPOSED
REMEDIES

George now proceeded to confront the plethora of proposed remedies to the enigma he had undertaken to unravel, namely the advance of poverty in lockstep with material progress.

The first of those purported remedies is "Greater Economy in Government."

"Now, there seems to be an evident connection between the immense sums thus taken from the people and the privations of the lower classes, and it is upon a superficial view natural to suppose that a reduction in the enormous burdens thus uselessly imposed would make it easier for the poor to make a living. But a consideration of the matter in the light of the economic principles heretofore traced out will show that this would not be the effect. A reduction in the amount taken from the aggregate produce of a community for taxation would be simply equivalent to an increase in the power of net production. It would in effect add to the productive power of labor just as do the increasing density of population and improvement in the arts. And as the advantage in one case goes, and must go, to the owners of land, in increased rent, so would the advantage in the other," observed George.

Clearly, the remedy did not lie in greater governmental economy.

"This argument for greater improvement in prosperity through tax relief is a persistent one on the part of business interests; it is one rarely advanced by the working poor, and certainly not by those on public assistance or those temporarily unemployed."

On those occasions when business interests and the wealthy have been granted tax relief, the ensuing bulge in capital investment and consumer spending have only had the effect of increasing the percentage of the nation's income and wealth in the hands of the wealthiest segment of the population. This, of course, still evades the question of the unsupported argument by George of the common interests of labor and capital vis a vis land.

"The second of these purported remedies is "The Diffusion of Education and Improved Habits of Industry and Thrift."

George asserted that, "There is, and always has been, a widespread belief among the more comfortable classes that the poverty and suffering of the masses are due to their lack of industry, frugality, and intelligence. This belief, which at once soothes the sense of responsibility and flatters by its suggestion of superiority, is probably even more prevalent in countries like the United States, where all men are politically equal, and where, owing to the newness of society, the differentiation into classes has been of individuals rather than families, than it is in older countries, where the lines of separation have been longer, and more sharply drawn.

"But whoever has grasped the laws of distribution of wealth, as in previous chapters they have been traced out, will see the mistake in this notion. The fallacy is similar to that which would be involved in the assertion that every one of a number of competitors might win a race. That any one might is true; that every one might is impossible.

"For, as soon as land acquires value, wages, as we have seen, do not depend upon the real earnings or product of labor, but upon what is left to labor after rent is taken out; and when land is monopolized, as it is everywhere except in the newest communities, rent must drive wages down to the point at which the poorest paid class will be just be able to live and reproduce, and thus wages are forced down to a minimum fixed by what is called the standard of comfort—that is, the amount of necessaries and comforts which habit leads the working classes to demand as the lowest on which they will consent to maintain their numbers. This being the case, industry, skill, frugality and intelligence can avail the individual only so far as they are superior to the general level—just as in a race speed can avail the runner only in so far as it exceeds that of his competitors...

"If, under existing conditions, American mechanics would come down to the Chinese standard of living, they would ultimately have come down to the Chinese standard of wages; or if English laborers would content themselves with the rice diet and scanty clothing of the Bengalee, labor would soon be as ill paid in England as in Bengal...

"It is true that greater industry and skill, greater prudence, and a higher intelligence are, as a rule, found associated with a better material condition of the working classes; but that this is effect, not cause, is shown by the relation of the facts. Wherever the material condition of the working classes has been improved, improvement in their personal qualities has followed, and wherever their material condition has been depressed, deterioration in these qualities has been the result"

The third of these purported remedies is "Combination of Workmen."

George dismisses the possibility of such remedy as follows;

"To raise wages in a particular occupation or occupations, which is all any combination of workmen yet made has been equal to attempting, is manifestly a task the difficulty of which progressively increases. For the higher are wages of any particular kind raised above their normal level with other wages, the stronger are the tendencies to bring them back. Thus, if a printers' union by a successful or threatened strike, raises the wages of typesetting by ten percent above the normal rate as compared to other wages, relative demand and supply are at once affected. On the one hand, there is a tendency to diminution of the amount of typesetting called for; and on the other, the higher rate of wages tends to increase the number of compositors in ways the strongest combination cannot altogether prevent.

"The only way by which wages could be raised to any extent and with any permanence by this method would be by a general combination, such as was aimed at by the Internationals, which would include laborers of all kinds. But such a combination may be set down as practically impossible, for the difficulties of combination, great enough in the most highly paid and smallest trades, become greater and greater as we descend in the industrial scale."

George now continued to insist that labor and capital were equal victims of the tendency of rent to sweep away all gains in productivity, as stated here, "If the contest were between labor and capital, it would be on much more equal terms. For **the power of capital to stand out is only some little greater than that of labor.** Capital not only ceases to earn anything when not used, but it goes to waste—for in nearly all its forms it can be maintained only by constant reproduction."

Observe once again George's consistent view of the equality or near-equality of the power of labor and capital.

The fourth putative remedy, as described by George, is "Cooperation."

George dismisses cooperation as a remedy as follows:

"Waiving all the difficulties that under present conditions beset cooperation either of supply or production, and supposing it so extended as to supplant present methods—that cooperative stores made the connection between producer and consumer with the minimum of expenses, and cooperative workshops, factories, farms and mines, abolished the employing capitalist who pays fixed wages, and greatly increased the efficiency of labor—what then? Why, simply that it would become possible to produce the same amount of wealth with less labor, and consequently that the owners of land, the source of all wealth, could command a greater amount of wealth for the use of their land. This is not a mere matter of theory; it is proved by experience and existing facts. Improved methods and improved machinery have the same effect that cooperation aims at—reducing the cost of bringing commodities to the consumer and increasing the efficiency of labor...But, as experience has amply shown, improvement in the methods and machinery of production and exchange have no tendency to improve the conditions of the lowest class, and wages are lower and poverty deeper where exchange goes on at the minimum of cost and production has the benefit of the best machinery. The advantage but adds to the rent...

"And the truth is that, except possibly in educational effects, cooperation can produce no general results that competition will not produce. Just as the cheaper-for-cash stores have a similar effect upon prices as the cooperative supply association, so does competition in production lead to a similar adjustment of forces and division of proceeds as would cooperative production. That increasing productive power does not add to the reward of labor, is not because of competition, but because competition is one sided. Land, without which there can be no production, is monopolized, and the competition of producers for its use forces wages to a minimum and gives all the advantage of increasing productive power to landowners in higher rents and increased land values."

The fifth ostensible remedy which George examined and rejected was "Governmental Direction and Interference."

He wrote, "As to truths that are involved in socialistic ideas I shall have something to say hereafter; but it is evident that whatever savors of regulation and restriction is in itself bad, and should not be resorted to if any other mode of accomplishing the same end presents itself...

"We have passed out of the socialism of the tribal state, and cannot enter it again except by a regression that would involve anarchy and perhaps barbarism. Our governments, as is already plainly evident, would break down in the attempt.

"Instead of an intelligent award of duties and earnings, we should have a Roman distribution of Sicilian corn, and the demagogue would soon become the Imperator.

"The ideal of Socialism is grand and noble; and it is, I am convinced, possible of realization; but such a state of society cannot be manufactured—it must grow. Society is an organism, not a machine. It can live only the individual life of its parts."

These remarks represent the essential political position of Henry George, a position Karl Marx is reputed to have found absurd.

The sixth presumptive solution, that of "More General Distribution of Land," appears to fly in the face of the natural tendency for land to coalesce into larger and larger holdings in response to technological advances which thereby achieve greater aggregate production.

"Let us abandon all attempts to get rid of the evils of land monopoly by restricting land ownership. An equal distribution of land is impossible, and anything short of that would be only a mitigation, not a cure, and a mitigation that would prevent the adoption of a cure. Nor is any remedy worth considering that does not fall in with the current of the times. That concentration is the order of development there can be no mistaking—the concentration of people in large cities, the concentration of handicrafts in large factories, the concentration of transportation by railway and steamship lines, and agricultural operations in large fields.

"All the currents of the time run to concentration. To resist it successfully we must throttle steam and discharge electricity from human service," concluded George.

21

THE UNPAIRING OF LABOR AND CAPITAL

Having alluded on several occasions to Henry George's undeviating pairing of labor and capital as equal victims of land's exploitation, and having questioned George's failure to recognize the growing power and dominance of capital even in his own time, this is perhaps the appropriate point to examine that question—prior to presenting George's "true remedy."

The means and manner by which rent has been traditionally justified—primarily on the basis of the differing productive capacities of privately owned land and the virtually uniform wages of agricultural workers in undefined proximities, with the extension of the meaning to all physical endowments, would appear at first to place land in an indisputably dominant and unassailable position as an agent of production.

However, as has previously been described in these pages, the advent of the factory, capable of emplacement on a relatively insignificant parcel of land (even wasteland unsuited for agriculture), and capable of producing with a relatively large labor force, wealth far greater than such small parcel of agricultural land might produce, could only signal the beginning of the end of agricultural land's domination of capital.

Of course, the capital required to construct and equip even the most primitive factory, one powered by an adjacent brook or river, required capital which could only be in the hands of landowners and mercantilists. Landowners who could foresee the benefits of investing in ocean spanning ships presumably could envision the great wealth producing capacity of early factories.

The literature of eighteenth and nineteenth century Britain and Europe is filled with tales of the early struggle between the class of aristocratic landowners and mercantilist and manufacturing upstarts. The literature of the latter part of the nineteenth century begins to illustrate the union of aristocratic landowning and new manufacturing and transporting classes through marriage.

The South of the United States, where aristocratic land owning dominance persisted, while the manufacturing and transporting classes flourished in the North, was undoubtedly the victim of a profitable but regressive retention of an economy and culture which was experienced as a threat to the new capitalist economy and culture of the North.

From the vantage point of the present, when the power and sway of capital is so obviously dominant, with funds in the trillions of dollars sloshing daily over the globe, It is almost inconceivable that labor and capital could have been viewed as virtually co-equal even in George's day.

The reason why George consistently rejected the obvious fact that capital was emerging as a force greater than that of land or labor can only be conjectured. It may have been due to his own experiences in California as well as the persistent dominance of the land factor in wealth production in much of the Old World, including Ireland, India, Russia, the American West, etc. It is also known that he possessed an innate dubiousness of Socialism as a solution to the problem which vexed him. This dubiousness could well have blinded him to the negative aspects of capital, as he lauded its progressive contributions.

Whatever the reason was for this great oversight, capital cannot (and actually could not in George's time) be overlooked as a factor contributing to the growth of wealth and poverty simultaneously.

Capital consists of impressed labor upon land or upon the worked up products of land. It therefore carries with it the capability of accumulation, despite its consistent amortization. It is a form of wealth used to create more wealth, and is readily reconverted to wealth. It should then, even in principle, be no surprise that wealth as capital can be aggregated from generation to generation, unless or until depleted by warfare or great natural catastrophes.

That capital (as with all wealth), is a hybrid of land and labor, is indicative if the great and growing importance of non-agricultural land in wealth production in the era of capital dominance. Of course, without labor, capital is impotent.

The development of society, where the vast bulk of labor is employed in manufacturing, points out not only the salient function of capital, but the replacement of the dominance of the landowner over labor with that of the owners of capital. It was the rise of a whole new class of labor, industrial labor, which led to the development of organized labor and a working class movement.

But the purpose of our inquiry here is to determine whether, and if so, in what degree the great discoveries of George, from correct definitions of economic terms; through impeachment of the wages fund theory (with all its implications); to the theory of marginal cultivation (or production) yielding a larger and larger percentage of production to landowners, including the rise of absolute (as opposed to percentile) increased produce to labor; and explanation of the reasons for periodic speculation and retrenchment; have application to the era of capitalist domination.

If this cannot be done, then George's brilliant analysis of progress and poverty in a predominantly agricultural era of production, will necessarily remain a brilliant commentary on post-feudal land policies and practices.

Let us begin with a re-examination of the diagram in, page 52, representing the progressive increase of rent (and diminution of wages and capital) as the margin of cultivation (or production) diminishes with expansion due to natural circumstances.

Since, as we have observed and determined, the return to capital with natural expansion has not diminished, but vastly increased over time, the diagram therefore cannot be applicable to capital (inclusive with or independent of the return to labor.) Can it, however, being a function of land (as well as labor) be placed above the margin of cultivation in a fusion with land? If this were so, then the ever-decreasing proportionate return to the third element of production, namely labor, would be consistently and progressively diminished with increased productivity, in accordance with the same diagram.

Both Malthus and Ricardo have written of the "natural wages" of laborers being only that which would sustain them to reproduce their own. Marx predicted that the natural development of capitalism would ultimately achieve the same result. Yet, we have witnessed a persistent if unsteady rise in the standard of living of people in the industrial world.

Now, George brilliantly observed that with rapid development, although the PROPORTION of overall production returned to labor plus capital would in the normal course of events be reduced, the ABSOLUTE quantity might well increase. This could account for the periodic rise in the standard of living coincidental with the expansion of production due to technological and administrative innovations.

It is also possible that contemporary capital, having become indistinguishable from land, functions as land in the diagrammatic representation of George's theory.

Three factors would appear to support such a view:

(a) periodic speculative surges in land value

(b) prosperous periods followed by recessions or depressions

(c) the almost persistent shift of increasing national wealth and income into fewer and fewer hands, as a percentage of population

These phenomena are integral parts of George's explanation of the progression of poverty with progress.

A clear distinction between labor in the establishment of George's theory and that which occurred during the rise of capitalist production is that of the diversity and mobility of labor. The entire theory of rent is represented in the previously referenced diagram, and is dependent upon virtually uniform wages in a proximate but indeterminate area, and the virtual immobility of labor due to its great impoverishment, not to speak of other coercions and bondages. Labor under a capitalist regime is necessarily highly diversified and far more mobile.

While this distinction would appear to weaken the accepted theory of rent, it never-the-less functions as an effective actual economic factor presently.

22

CAPITAL AND LAND ACTING SIMILARLY

Capital, being wealth intended for creating more wealth, is in fact crystallized labor and land or worked up land (with land defined as all natural endowments). For the purpose of examining capital AS LAND, in the Georgian sense, it is useful to set aside thoughts of agricultural land. This "land," endowment of nature, cannot be made by man; labor applied to it mindfully creates wealth.

This wealth is translatable to capital, which needs to be replenished, but does not diminish in value in the sense that the extraction of copper ore, for example, from a mine does. Once the mine is depleted of its ore, the remaining land has virtually no economic value.

Following the era of George's formulation of his theory, land, which had been the basis (with labor} for virtually all wealth from time immemorial, began to yield to capital as a force in wealth production. Iron mines were appropriated by the owners of iron and steel mills, not vice versa; millers and manufacturers of food grains began to dominate the farmers producing such grains; canners and distributors of products of the sea were soon dominating the fishing fleets harvesting the "land." Capital was clearly in the ascendancy, although nothing can be made into wealth without land (as natural endowment).

By its very nature, the products of land, raw materials such as coal, oil, ores; waterfalls suitable for energy production, fishing banks, even elevated sites suitable for capturing wind power, were simply situated in a dispersed competitive market. The capacity for market hegemony or cartelization was virtually nil.

However, in respect to any central consuming market, each such natural endowment played a similar role to agricultural land demanding rent on the basis of high productivity. The most productive coal mine, for example, could command the highest "rent" (actually income), based upon the margin of productivity of other coal mines, wherever situated, once labor and shipping costs were incorporated in the productivity of the more distant mine.

It is here suggested that the margin of productivity concept is equally applicable to capital, and the diagram constructed showing the return to more highly productive lands producing a greater return as the margin of productivity in a community expands, effects the return to capital identically. Clearly, capital is in higher demand at the core of an expanding community, which has increased its economic product in consequence of concentration of population, enriched infrastructure, greater division of labor, etc. than in the newer areas. Capital should be in higher demand in the course of development in the vital center than in outlying areas, producing the same phenomena as is the case with agricultural land, the exception being where government in effect supports a higher return on capital, such as with military or insurance protection in distant lands, where the return to capital represents virtual expropriation by capital.

Since capital is in such significant measure land, it should not be surprising that the above is so; and that its accretion is primarily due to its land content may be seen in the constant input of labor required to maintain it against erosion and a return to original "land."

It may now be more clearly seen why both land and capital, as the economic community expands, command a larger and larger share of overall production, tending generally to a diminished percentile share for labor—but providing for an absolute improvement in the return to labor when production expands dramatically, despite this trend, when a reduced percentile share constitutes an absolute increase as compared to a prior return.

Essentially, this observation supports the theories of those seeking land reform and those seeking capitalist reform.

It must be remembered that whatever laws of the distribution of production between land, labor, and capital may be developed, such laws must be equally applicable to where only land and labor are engaged in production, since the earliest production was without capital.

The foregoing analysis of the similarities in the manner of extraction of income by land and capital (despite their differences in capacity) leads us into a clearer understanding of economic developments of the past century and a quarter

While land (in the agricultural sense) is subject to the law of diminishing returns, this is not true of industrial production, as agricultural production is limited by the amount of labor which can be efficiently employed. Industrial production is capable of producing far greater wealth than can be derived from agricultural land, and virtually without limit. However, industrial production, in advancing so greatly in progressive societies, has made itself increasingly hostage to wealth in the form of mineral land—especially fuels, so indispensable to manufacturing and transport.

The author believes that, utilizing the Georgian method of analysis of wealth distribution, he has made an organic transition from exclusionary emphasis upon land to the capitalistic organization of production, bearing in mind the pivotal role of non-agricultural land.

The author has striven to show the analogous behavior of both land and capital in extracting a growing percentage of product and leaving labor with a smaller percentile share of increased production, which may on occasion be an increased absolute quantity. The essential basis for this postulation is that both land and capital are assets which demand in return for their utilization, not only the original utilized, undiminished asset, but a "rental" for such use. In this effort he has attempted to erect a bridge over the boundary within which Henry George strove to shield capital from analysis and criticism. This has been done utilizing the analytical system developed by George himself.

We are now free to examine capitalism as an organic outgrowth of the pre-capitalist agricultural system of production, with its unique and powerful capacity to provide a virtual cornucopia of wealth.

But before doing so, it will be instructive to examine the theories of wealth production and distribution of those who preceded not only Henry George, but Adam Smith as well

23

HISTORICAL ECONOMICS

The end of the 16th century witnessed the weakening hold of the Church's "just price" as the prevailing rule in economic exchange, concurrent with the burgeoning role of mercantilist trading internationally. The accumulation of wealth in the hands of these mercantilists, as well as in the Church's coffers, made possible the beginnings of small capitalist enterprise, which soon led to academic speculations by scholars and merchants.

Antoyne de Chretien, in 1615, coined the term "political economy," as he ventured to elevate the profit motive in the face of increasingly clear church hypocrisy in nominal opposition to profit and usury while engaged in exploitation of the vast new lands of the New World.

Much study and a large body of written work soon followed through the 17th century, and well into the 18th century prior to the Advent of Adam Smith's major works. During the intervening century and a half between Montchretien and Smith, the pattern of economic thought and speculation generally endorsed the current economic developments toward capital accumulation, ventured to find fault with certain theoretical constructs, or challenged these constructs with evidence of contemporary experience.

As an example of the latter, one cannot ignore the writings of P. Boisguillebert in 1697, in which he provides an almost modern description of the onset of crisis and depression. And financial crises were by no means unknown prior to the time and work of Adam Smith, as the economic writings of Richard Cantillon are informed by his personal experience of the financial collapse in Paris in 1720, the same year which witnessed the implosion of the Great South Sea bubble in London.

Through the latter part of the seventeenth century, Sir William Petty, a man of extraordinary scholarship and worldly accomplishments, advanced the notion of: the labor theory of value, surplus value, differential rent, the theory of interest, the distinction between price and value, the role of monopolies, the velocity of circulation, the multiplier effect, natural law, national accounting, division of labor and economies of scale, and public works as a remedy for unemployment.

One may well ask, what was there left for Adam Smith to discover around 1775, and why is the name William Petty virtually unknown, while that of Adam Smith's is universally celebrated? Petty's studies and theories were all the more remarkable in that the Industrial Revolution was as yet unborn.

One might venture to suggest that Adam Smith's philosophy, as incoherent as it was, was in all likelihood totally compatible with the requirements of the burgeoning industrial capitalist class.

Smith, building upon the prior writings of Richard Cantillon in mid-eighteenth century, advanced the now defunct notion of the "wages fund," which provided the ideological basis for Malthus' infamous doctrine justifying the virtual periodic genocide of the working population of England. It wasn't until the utter demolition of this clergyman's mathematical perversions by Henry George in the latter third of the nineteenth century that the pious executioner's justification for gross iniquity in the distribution of the rapidly enlarging national wealth was consigned to the rubbish heap of history. And yet, it still persists in the thinking of the public, and insinuates itself into contemporary political argument. Henry George, in demolishing the so-called mathematics of Malthus in his *PROGRESS AND POVERTY,* managed in that same book to impeach Smith's endorsement of the "wages fund."

Among Smith's other errors and contradictions:

1. The cost of production is made up of rent, wages, interest, and profit. Inasmuch as the factors of production are solely, land, labor, and capital, respectively returning rent, wages, and interest, profit is extraneous, itself breaking down into wages of superintendence, compensation for risk, and interest for borrowed capital. Profit cannot be regarded as a factor of production , as it is not an a priori cost, and may not even come into existence in due course.

2. He regarded "services" as unproductive. Indeed the maintenance and repair of a machine is held to be productive, but the maintenance and repair of a workman by a physician, utilizing said machine, is held unproductive. Such folly still persists in our present tax code, where expenses related to business income production are wholly deductible and the individual's medical expenses to maintain his or her productive life are severely limited

3. For Smith, savings equated to investing. The views of others that savings did not automatically translate into investment where economic troubles loomed hardly entered into his consciousness, so much faith had he in the machine model that he constructed in his head.

4. On the one hand, Smith regarded all government expenditure as unproductive; on the other, he considered the proper role of the state to be no more than: A—national defense, B—defense of the rich against the poor, C—erection and maintenance of public institutions and works. Contradictory, but consistently in the service of his emerging capitalist industrialist benefactors, while mollifying the great land owning and merchant families.

5. Smith favored a legal ceiling on the rate of interest. Some free marketeer! He also favored progressive taxation. Some conservative!

6. Smith believed that government expenditure could do nothing to raise the level of employment. Others were advocating that, inasmuch as the destitute and able-bodied would have to be sustained in any event, they be employed in public work. Had he lived in the 1930's, God knows what he would have advocated.

Other political economists followed hard on the heels of the great "synthesizer," differed little or greatly with Smith's constructs and judgments, which they regarded as largely deduced from his idiosyncratic views of human economic behavior. Simon de Sismondi did not believe in the self-regulating capacity of laissez-faire (anticipating Keynes); and W. Thompson reverted to the ancient "labor theory" of value in affirming the rightful claims of labor to the WHOLE product of industry. K. Marx would reiterate that same claim toward the end of the nineteenth century. Thompson went so far as to enunciate the heresy of heresies, namely that "man can, indeed, be miserable with goods in superfluity, and comparatively happy with a small portion."

Malthus, the priestly mathematician, and Ricardo, the stockbroker logician, established the format for modern economists. Economic reality scarcely informed their cerebral constructs as each fabricated elaborate theoretical formulations, mathematically buttressed, to disguise their essential purpose of serving and justifying their patrons' interests while inflating their own intellectual credits.

The secular priesthood interpreting and promoting the material world of industrial capitalism, in contrast to the clerical world of the church, was waxing apace with spreading capitalism. Having served their masters in propounding theories and interpretations of theories initially (they were always in the train of merchants and industrialists, who had no intention of awaiting ideological justification), their numbers and influence in universities, government, banks, insurance companies, and financial institutions such as brokerage houses swelled to a flood. Until Karl Marx, Henry George, and Thorstein Veblen, serious criticism of the failure of capitalism to reduce, let alone eliminate, poverty at a time of enormous material growth, were virtually non-existent.

Marx propounded the inherent contradictions of capitalism, these contradictions requiring the impoverishment and alienation of an entire working class, and necessitating imperialistic rivalries to export "surplus value" stolen from the working class, with these rivalries necessarily leading to wars. Greed, economic rivalries, and warfare certainly were nothing new, even if certain methods of production and inequitable distribution were new. The remedy of the workers' ownership of the means of production (capital), being only conceptual, did not permit of examination of any real world models, with such inherent contradictions that might also reveal themselves. There had been peasant rebellions under feudalism, sometimes led by disaffected priests, and the fiery priesthood of a son of the bourgeoisie was probably inevitable.

Henry George, originally a printer and journalist, deducing from his California land experience the primacy of "land" in the triumvirate of land, labor, and capital as the factors of production, brilliantly and passionately utilized the methodology of Ricardo in identifying the reasons for poverty accompanying progress disproportionately. The theories and rationalizations of virtually all political economists preceding his were systematically dismantled, while he offered a non-revolutionary reform to grave injustice.

The essential features which virtually all economic theorists shared were the following

(1) Each sought to explain in conceptual and abstract terms the reality which he observed. Economic development did not wait upon these theoretical constructs, but proceeded with its own internal logic and dynamic.

(2) Each political economist perceived the economic system in which he lived from the point of view of his placement within it, his dependency upon those who effectively dominated and controlled it, as filtered through his own temperament and personality.

(3) The earliest attempts to rationalize the workings of the economic society emerging from feudalism, particularly

as the church's hold on the economic life of society weakened , were directed to an essentially agricultural society emerging from feudalism. Land and labor were the predominant factors of production, with the modest quantity of capital participating in production (and therefore receiving the return of interest) absolutely minimal.

(4) While at the outset of economic development in Europe, land was held almost entirely by an aristocracy which controlled its use absolutely; this same aristocracy held their laborers in bondage virtually to the same degree. It was only with the growth of chartered towns, guilds of artisans, and the lessening bondage of labor that the factors enabling development out of stasis could begin.

24

THE CASE AGAINST PRIVATE OWNERSHIP OF LAND

Having meticulously dispatched every remedy propounded for the amelioration of poverty concurrent with progress, George then proceeded to inveigh against "the injustice of private property in land." This he undertook to do in great detail in order to clear the ground for proposing his own remedy, one which would meet the tests of justice and practicality, which could be put into practice without recourse to violence. Of this remedy, more later; but first it is necessary to present George's arguments challenging every private title in land as providing an insight into his vision of the grave and disastrous consequences of private property in land upon social stability throughout history and up to the time of his writing. Clearly, to establish that private property in land has led to the destruction of every prior civilization could only buttress his remedy, if provable on its own merits.

The essence of his argument, elaborated upon at length, is that, "There can be to the ownership of anything no rightful title which is not derived from the title of the man to himself. There can be no other rightful title because (1st) there is no other natural right from which any other title can be derived, and (2nd) because the recognition of any other title is inconsistent with and destructive of this."

He continued with, "The right of ownership that springs from labor excludes the possibility of any other right of ownership. If a man is rightfully entitled to the produce of his labor, then no one can be rightfully entitled to the ownership of anything which is not the product of his labor, or the labor of someone else from whom the right has passed to him. If production give to the producer the right to exclusive possession and enjoyment, there can rightfully be no exclusive possession and enjoyment of anything not the production of labor, and the recognition of private property in land is a wrong."

George held that whatever might be said for the institution of private property in land, it was plain that it could not be defended on the score of justice. He was quite passionate on that score, his passion fueling the power of his arguments.

"The equal right of all men to the use of land is as clear as their equal right to breathe the air—it is a right proclaimed by the fact of their existence. For we cannot suppose that some men have a right to be in this world and others no right."

For the purpose of this study, George's remedy, and arguments supporting his remedy, are of particular significance in their presumptive relevance to capital behaving as land in the division and distribution of productive output.

In a continuing demolition of the right or justice of private property in land, George advanced the argument that slavery itself is the natural and inevitable consequence of private property in land. For what purpose were captives (almost always in consequence of war for the acquisition or dominion of land) spared, except that they might be employed on land acquired or long held? Serfdom in all its forms in medieval Europe, while originally a contract between baron and original land holder for security in exchange for labor or produce, metamorphosed into the security of bondage, with land, labor, and laborer himself ultimately possessions of the lord. From time immemorial, with the beginning of the tillage of land, land was held in common, with evidence up to recent times of the annual rotation of strips of land of differing fertility among families engaged in tilling common lands. Common lands in England, for example, were available for the pasturing of privately owned live-stock until such lands were expropriated by Henry VIII for gifting to his cronies and allies in an act of outright thievery. Such lands still remain the property of the families of those beneficiaries of Henry's perverse largesse. The transition from tribal (common) ownership of land extends even further back in history.

In recognition of the evils deriving from private ownership of land, wise and judicious men such has Herbert Spencer and John Stuart Mill have advocated that means be sought for restoring land to common ownership by means of compensation to present day landowners at the expense of the entire nation. A similar, but differing, scheme was resorted to by the British government in liberation of slaves in the British West Indies by compensating slave owners at public expense in the sum of one hundred million dollars. It was just such a scheme of slave owner compensation for the liberation of slaves in the South of the United States (primarily) which President Lincoln offered in an effort to avert the oncoming Civil War. As a practical matter, in no wise buttressing the justice of such financial compensation for the release of slaves, market purchase of all slaves held in the South for emancipation by the proceeds of a Federal bond issue (rejected by the South) would certainly have been far, far cheaper in treasure and lives than that consumed in the Civil War.

But George saw in such "compensation" the perpetuation of the original and continuing injustice, whereby, in effect, the state would become the perpetual lease holder of the land of the nation, while assuming the payment of rent from the national income. In his view, no abrogation of the advance of poverty with progress could occur through such "compensation."

In support of his rejection of any compensation to the owners of land despite the myriad of cases where land had been purchased with resources derived from honest industry and trading, George made reference to the common law treatment of land found to be held with a defective title. However long held, and whatever the degree and manner of improvements made upon such land by the landholder in good faith, the court will strip him of his land and improvements for return to the person who holds an unblemished title. The common law, which is the basis for such draconian treatment, and is itself the fruit of landowner acceptance and experience, George would apply to all privately owned land as defective in title and rightfully returnable to original common ownership. He would, however, make no claim on legitimate improvements to such lands.

In further buttressing the remedy he proposed to offer for ameliorating the underlying injustice of privately owned land, George then proceeded to review the phenomenon of private property in land from a historical perspective.

In a powerful and scarcely impeachable historical review of land ownership, George delineated the ancient roots of common ownership of land and its usurpation to private ownership through the centuries.

"The 'sacredness of property' has been preached so constantly and effectively by those 'conservators of ancient barbarism,' as Voltaire styled the lawyers, that most people look upon private ownership of land as the very foundation of civilization, and if the resumption of land as common property is suggested, think of it at first blush either as chimerical vagary, which never has and never can be realized, or as a proposition to overturn society from its base and bring about a reversion to barbarism.

"If it were true that land had always been treated as private property, that would not prove the justice or necessity of continuing so to treat it, any more than the universal existence of slavery, which might once have been safely affirmed, would prove the justice or necessity of making property of human flesh and blood," George wrote at the outset of his historical review. He continued thusly:

"The observations of travelers, the researches of the critical historians, who within a recent period have done so much to reconstruct the forgotten records of the people, the investigations of such men as Sir Henry Maine, Emile de Laveleye, Professsor Nasse of Bonn, and others, into the growth of institutions, prove that wherever human society has formed, the common right of men to the use of the earth has been recognized, and that nowhere has unrestricted individual ownership been freely adopted. Historically, as ethically, private property in land is robbery. It nowhere springs from contract; it can nowhere be traced to perceptions of justice or expediency; it has everywhere had its birth in war and conquest, and in the selfish use which the cunning have made of superstition and law.

"Even where the development of agriculture had imposed the necessity of recognizing exclusive possession of land in order to secure the exclusive enjoyment of the results of the labor expended in cultivating it, the division of land between working units, whether families, joint families, or individuals, went only as far as necessary for that purpose, with pasture and forest lands retained as common, and equality as to agricultural land being secured either by periodic redivision or rotation."

In George's view, the causes for the transition from common property in land to private property in land could be summarized as residing in the concentration of power in the hands of chieftains and the military class, consequent on a state of warfare, which enabled them to monopolize common land; the effect of conquest in reducing the conquered to a state of predial slavery, and dividing their lands among the conquerors, and in disproportionate share to the chiefs.

George held that it was the struggle between the idea of equal rights to the soil and the tendency to monopolize it in individual possession that caused the internal conflicts of Greece and Rome; and it was the check given to this tendency—in Greece by such institutions as those of Lycurgus and Solon, and in Rome by the Licinian Law and subsequent division of land that gave to each their days of strength and glory; and it was the final triumph of this tendency that destroyed both.

Great estates ruined Greece, as afterward great estates ruined Italy.

In a brief digression, the author would point out in further support of his (the author's) contention that, as economic and social factors, land and capital perform similarly, even in their tendency toward monopolization and its inevitable consequences.

George then went on to describe the reasons why in the era of "natural rights" inhering to the private property produced by one's own labor, these same rights should have been ascribed to private property in land. In his view, the progress of civilization had the tendency to diminish or abolish the grosser forms of supremacy connected with land ownership, or to make them less obvious, and landowners were thus easily enabled to put property in land on the same basis as other property. Also, the growth of national power, either in the form of royalty or parliamentary power, stripped the great lords of individual power and importance, and of their jurisdiction and power over persons, and in so repressing striking abuses, contributed to drawing away attention from the essential injustice involved in private property in land. What ultimately broke the power of the landed barons was the rise and growth of the artisan and trading classes, which held strongly to the principle of "natural rights," rights which chastened great landowners were more than pleased to appropriate as applying to their holdings.

25

PRIVATE PROPERTY IN LAND AND THE U.S.A.

George dealt with land as private property in the United States as a special case, writing:

"Had the circumstances which beset the first English settlers in North America been such as to call their attention de novo to the question of land ownership there can be no doubt that they would have reverted to first principles, just as they reverted to first principles in matters of government; and individual land ownership would have been rejected, just as aristocracy and monarchy were rejected. But while in the country from which they came this system had not yet fully developed itself, nor its effects been fully felt, the fact that in the new country an immense continent invited settlement prevented any question of the justice and policy of new private property in land from arising. For in a new country, equality seems sufficiently assured if no one is permitted to take land to the exclusion of the rest. At first no harm seems to be done by treating land as absolute property. There is plenty of land left for those who choose to take it, and the slavery that in a later stage of development necessarily springs from the individual ownership of land is not felt."

In a larger sense, the discovery of the New World had an immense impact upon the relationship of land to labor throughout North and South America as well as the western European states which had engaged in exploration and discovery.

The Spanish and Portuguese discoveries in central and South America were claimed in the names of the respective kings, confirmed by the Pope, and divided into immense tracts as grants to privileged aristocrats and courtiers of the kings. The treasures initially sought were precious metal which could readily be confiscated and sent back to Europe to justify the costs of exploration and evoke the pleasure and indulgence of the European monarchs. It was only subsequently that the land itself and the indigenous population as potential slave labor were seen as the true treasure. Haciendas, much like the Roman latifundia, and worked by slave labor, soon followed.

In the parts of British America later to be called New England, settlers were in large measure religious refugees who struggled for survival in a harsh, new environment among native peoples upon whom they had frequently to rely to fend off starvation; simple homesteads capable of family tillage was the rule.

In Virginia and to the South, where the settlement had an aristocratic character, the immense land grants by the English Crown required an imported labor force suited to the extreme heat of the summer growing season. As the sparse Indian population could in no way be induced or forced to work the land, the importation of African slaves became the means to create new English latifundia.

The initial impact upon the Spanish economy by the influx of Aztec and Inca gold, was an increase in the price of everything in Spain; but within a century, or thereabouts, the beginnings of significant migration to the New World began to decrease the pressure of population toward less and less productive lands with a decline in the margin of cultivation responsible for increasing depredations of rent.

"The American people have failed to see the essential injustice of property in land because, as yet, they have not felt its full effects. This public domain—the vast extent of land yet to be reduced to private possession, the enormous common to which the faces of the energetic were always turned, has been the great fact that, since the days when the first settlements began to fringe the Atlantic Coast, has formed our national character and colored our national thought. It is not that we have eschewed a titled aristocracy and abolished primogeniture; that we elect all our officers from school director up to President; that our laws run in the name of the people, instead of in the name of a prince; that the state knows no religion, and our judges wear no wigs - that we have been exempted from the ills that Fourth of July orators used to point to as characteristic of the effete despotisms of the Old World. The general intelligence, the general comfort, the active invention, the power of adaptation and assimilation , the free independent spirit, the energy and hopefulness that have marked our people, are not causes, but results—they have sprung from unfenced land," wrote George.

"The republic," he continued, "has entered upon a new era, an era in which the monopoly of land will tell with accelerating effect. The great fact which has been so potent is ceasing to be. The public domain is almost gone—a very few years will end its influence, already rapidly failing . For a long time to come there will be millions of acres of public lands carried on the books of the Land Department. But it must be remembered that the best part of the continent for agricultural purposes is already overrun, and that it is the poorest land that is left."

And then, "But the evil effects of making the land of a whole people the exclusive property of some do not wait for final appropriation of the public domain to show themselves. It is not necessary to contemplate them in the future; we may see them in the present. They have grown with our growth, and are still increasing.

"We plow our fields, we open new mines, we found new cities, we drive back the Indian and exterminate the buffalo, we girdle the land with iron roads and lace the air with telegraph wires; we add knowledge to knowledge, and utilize invention after invention; we build schools and endow colleges; yet it becomes no easier for the masses of our people to make a living. On the contrary, it is becoming harder. The wealthy class is becoming more wealthy; but the poorer class is becoming more dependent. The gulf between the employed and the employer is growing wider, social contrasts are becoming sharper; as liveried carriages appear, so do barefooted children. We are becoming used to talk of the working classes and the propertied classes: beggars are becoming so common that where it was once thought a crime little short of highway robbery to refuse food to one who asked for it, the gate is now barred and bulldog loosed, while laws are passed against vagrants which suggest those of Henry VIII.

"These are the results of private property in land—the effects of a principle that must act with increasing and increasing force."

26

THE BEST USE OF LAND

Before embarking on his remedy for the ills George laid upon land as private property, he argued strongly and persuasively that land as private property is inconsistent with the best use of land. The obverse of this thesis is among the strongest arguments advanced by the proponents of land as private property. Their argument is that land owned by all is inevitably neglected by all. It is the common and widely held belief that the individual owner of a parcel of land is the most productive producer, and contemporary experience with collective farm production in the former Soviet Union, versus the productivity of privately allowed lots there (as well as efforts at collectivizing land elsewhere), would appear to support that position conclusively. It must be noted, however, that the vastly greater productivity on allowed private lots was probably due to the lot holder's guarantee of ownership of his own improvements and produce under the title granted to his private dacha

However, George wrote, "There is a delusion resulting from the tendency to confound the accidental with the essential, a delusion which the law writers have done their best to extend, and political economists generally have acquiesced in, rather than endeavored to expose—that private property in land is necessary to the proper use of land, and to make land common property again would be to destroy civilization and revert to barbarism." Continuing, George asserted, "...it does not take a sage to see that what is required for the improvement of land is not absolute ownership of land, but security for the improvements. This will be obvious to whoever will look around him...among us, nothing is more common than for land to be improved by those who do not own it. The greater part of the land of Great Britain is cultivated by tenants, the greater part of the buildings of London are built upon leased ground, and even in the United States the same system prevails everywhere to a greater or less extent. Thus it is a common matter for use to be separated from ownership.

"Would not all this land be cultivated and improved just as well if the rent went to the state or municipality, as now, when it goes to private individuals? If no private ownership in land were acknowledged, but all land were held in this way, the occupier or user paying rent to the state, would not land be used and improved as well and as securely as now? There can be but one answer: of course it would. Then would the resumption of land as common property in no wise interfere with the proper use and improvement of land.

"It was for the sake of obtaining this security that, in the beginning of the feudal period so many of the smaller landholders surrendered the ownership of their land to a military chieftain, receiving back the use of them in fief or trust, and kneeling bareheaded before the lord, with their hands between his hands, swore to serve him with life, and limb, and worldly honor. Similar instances of giving up of ownership of land for the sake of security in its enjoyment are to be seen in Turkey, where a peculiar exemption from taxation and extortion attaches to Vakout, or church land, and where it is a common thing for a Landowner to sell his land to a mosque for a nominal price, with the understanding that he may remain a tenant upon it at a fixed rent.

"The complete recognition of common rights to land need in no way interfere with the complete recognition of individual right to improvement or produce. Two men may own a ship without sawing her in half. The ownership of a railway may be divided into a hundred thousand shares, and yet trains be run with as much system and precision as if there were but a single owner.

"So far from the recognition of private property in land being necessary to the proper use of land, the contrary is the case. Treating land as private property stands in the way of its proper use. Were land treated as public property it would be used and improved as there was need for its use or improvement, but being treated as private property, the individual owner is permitted to prevent others from using or improving what he cannot or will not use or improve himself.

"When the title is in dispute, the most valuable land lies unimproved for years; in many parts of England improvement is stopped because, the estates being entailed, no security to improvers can be given; and large tracts of land which, were they treated as public property, would be covered with buildings and crops, are kept idle to gratify the caprice of the owners."

The desperate plight of the Irish, driven in the hundreds of thousands from their homes and plots during the famine years in the eighteenth century, was due in large measure to the practice of "rent wracking" engaged in at this crucial time by the large land owners (Irish as well as English) who had abandoned the ancient practice of fixed tenure and fixed annual rent, which had fostered industry and improvement on the part of tenant farmers enjoying the virtual security of actual ownership

Under the new system, any farmer who gave evidence of income above that necessary for subsistence, not to speak of one so fortuitous and foolish as to reveal the same, soon found, upon renewal of his lease, his new rent raised to sweep away any increased income stemming from improvement of his lot.

Those landowners holding large estates were the descendants of lords who had been granted those lands by a monarch who came into possession of such lands by conquest, extortion, or other arrogation and claimed them as ultimate owner. Every single acre of English land was claimed by the Norman King William the Conqueror, as his singular possession, upon completion of the conquest of England in 1066. Vast areas were subsequently granted to his officers, allies, and aides, in return for established and acknowledged services and revenues. These enormous land grants were the basis for the English aristocracy, which still derives enormous rents from their properties. In point of fact, vast tracts of the land upon which London is built is still in the possession of the family of the Duke of Westminster, the first Duke having been William's Master of Horse.

Whether the sovereign is a king, in effect taxing the entire nation for his own benefit and riches, or a commonwealth taxing the entire nation for benefits to be dispersed back to the nation, the mechanism employed in the former case might just as readily be employed in the latter case to better purpose. In essence, such is the argument by George for the public ownership of land.

As to the benefits to be derived, without the chaos and injustices which would ensue in an effort to effect such a monumental change, George advanced his unique remedy, which captured the imagination of much of the world, until ridiculed and dismissed by vested interests.

27

LAND AS COMMON PROPERTY

Having established the essential injustice and dire consequences of private property in land, including increasing poverty among the working classes, recurring paroxysms of industrial depression, the scarcity of employment, the stagnation of capital, and the myriad of social ills stemming in consequence, George boldly asserted that he had explored all amelioration only to conclude that there was no remedy for the aforementioned evils but the abolition of their cause.

"```We have seen that private property in land has no warrant in justice, but stands condemned as the denial of natural right—a subversion of the law of nature that as social development goes on must condemn the masses of men to a slavery the hardest and most degrading.

"We have weighed every objection, and seen that neither on the ground of equity or expediency is there anything to deter us from making land common property by confiscating rent.

"But a question of method remains. How shall we do it?

"I do not propose either to purchase or confiscate private property in land. The first would be unjust; the second needless. Let the individuals who now hold it still retain, if they want to, possession of what they are pleased to call their land. Let them continue to call it their land. Let them buy and sell it, and bequeath and devise it. We may safely leave them the shell, if we take the kernel. It is not necessary to confiscate land; it is only necessary to confiscate rent.

"We already take some rent in taxation. We have only to make some changes in our modes of taxation to take it all," asserted George.

Where land is not rented out, but wholly improved and worked, individually or corporately, clearly it is land value which must be taxed to achieve the above stated goal.

Continuing, George wrote, "In this way the State may become the universal landlord without calling herself so, and without assuming a single new function. In form, the ownership of land would remain just as now. No owner of land need be dispossessed, and no restriction need be placed upon the amount of land any one could hold, for rent being taken by the state in taxes, land, no matter in whose name it stood, or in what parcels it is held, would be really common property, and every member of the community would participate in the advantages of its ownership.

"Now, insomuch as the taxation of rent, or land values must necessarily be increased just as we abolish other taxes, we may put the proposition into practical form by proposing—

TO ABOLISH ALL TAXATION SAVE THAT UPON LAND VALUES.

George now proposed to examine his remedy first by the canons of taxation.

"The best tax by which public revenues can be raised is evidently that which will closest conform to the following conditions:

1. That it bear as lightly as possible upon production—so as least to check the increase of the general fund from which taxes must be paid and the community maintained.

2. That it is easily and cheaply collected, and fall as directly as may be possible upon the ultimate payers—so as to take from the people as little as possible in addition to what it yields the government.

3. That it be certain—so as to give the least opportunity for tyranny or corruption on the part of officials, and the least temptation to law breaking and evasion on the part of taxpayers..

4. That it bear equally—so as to give no citizen an advantage or put any at a disadvantage, as compared with others."

George then proceeded to discuss each of the four characteristics in detail.

As regards the effect of taxes on production, he wrote, "All taxes must evidently come from the produce of land and labor, since there is no other source of wealth than the union of human exertion with material and the forces of nature

"The mode of taxation is, in fact, quite as important as the amount. As a small burden badly placed may distress a horse that could carry with ease a much larger one properly adjusted, so a people may be impoverished and their power of producing wealth destroyed by taxation, which, if levied in another way, could be borne with ease. A tax on date trees, imposed by Mohammed Ali, caused the Egyptian fellahs to cut down their trees; but a tax of twice the amount imposed on the land produced no such result. The tax of ten percent on all sales, imposed by the Duke of Alva in the Netherlands, would, had it been maintained, have all but stopped exchange while yielding but little revenue.

"...the great class of taxes from which revenue may be derived without interference with production are taxes upon monopolies— for the profit of monopoly is in itself a tax levied upon production, and to tax it is simply to divert into the public coffers what production must in any event pay.

"The value of land does not express the reward of production, as does the value of crops, of cattle, of buildings, or any of the things which are styled personal property and improvements. It is not in any case the creation of the individual who owns the land; it is created by the growth of the community. Hence the community can take it all without in any way lessening the incentive to improvement or in the slightest degree lessening the production of wealth. Taxes may be imposed on the value of land until all rent is taken by the State, without reducing the wages of labor or the reward of capital one iota; without increasing the price of a single commodity, or making production in any way more difficult..."

As regards the ease and cheapness of collection, George wrote:

"...as under all fiscal systems some part of the public revenues is collected from taxes on land, and the machinery for that purpose already exists and could as well be made to collect all as a part. The cost of collecting the revenue now obtained by other taxes might be entirely saved by substituting the tax on land values for all other taxes. What an enormous saving might thus be made can be inferred from the horde of officials now engaged in collecting these taxes...

"A tax on land values does not add to prices, and is thus paid directly by the persons on whom it falls; whereas, all taxes upon things of unfixed quantity increase prices, and in the course of exchange are shifted from seller to buyer, increasing as they go. If we impose a tax upon money loaned, as has been often attempted, the lender will charge the tax to the borrower, and the borrower must pay it or not obtain the loan. If the borrower uses it in his business, he in his turn must get back the tax from his customers, or his business becomes unprofitable..."

As regards certainty, George wrote:

"Certainty is an important element in taxation, for just as the collection of a tax depends upon the diligence and faithfulness of the collectors and the public spirit and honesty of those who are to pay it will opportunities for tyranny and corruption be opened on the one side, and for evasions and frauds on the other.

"The methods by which the bulk of our revenues are collected are condemned on this ground, if on no other. The gross corruptions and fraud occasioned in the United States by the whisky and tobacco taxes are well known; the constant underevaluations of the Custom House, the ridiculous untruthfulness of income tax returns, and the absolute impossibility of getting anything like a just valuation of personal property, are matters of notoriety..."

As regards equity, George wrote:

"Adam Smith speaks of incomes as 'enjoyed under the protection of the state'; and this is the ground upon which the equal taxation of all species of property is commonly insisted upon—that it is equally protected by the state. The basis of this idea is evidently that the enjoyment of property is made possible by the state - that there is a value created and maintained by the community, which is justly called upon to meet community expenses. Now of what values is this true? Only of the value of land. This is a value that does not arise until a community is formed, and that, unlike other values, grows with the growth of the community. It exists only as the community exists. Scatter again the largest community, and land, now so valuable, would have no value at all. With every increase of population the value of land rises, with every decrease it falls. This is true of nothing else save of things which, like the ownership of land, are in their nature monopolies."

28

THE ALTERED CHARACTER OF LAND

His inquiry into the phenomenon of increasing poverty concurrent with economic progress, now buttressed with undeniable proof that the former is in fact inseparable from the latter, Henry George then proceeded in the sequential roles of historian and philosopher.

In the rise and fall of all prior civilizations, he pointed to the destructive social, economic, and political consequences of the monopolization of land ownership by a dominant elite. In truth, his task of rigorously demonstrating the phenomenon suggested in the title of his masterpiece was concluded with the advocacy of his unique remedy (peaceful and generally beneficial confiscation of rent through taxation in replacement of all other taxes).

As has previously been indicated, the equating of labor and capital, even in Henry George's day, as joint victims of the depredations of rent, appear unsustainable. The subsequent dynamism of capitalism (a term scarcely employed in George's day), with capital subsuming the role of land, and the universal primacy of capital (even in so-called socialistic societies) cannot help but represent an evolution from the era of the primacy of land as natural endowment.

Here, however, a distinction in the several characters of "land" suggests itself. "Land" as agricultural and mineral source of food, fiber, and a whole variety of substances, may be, and indeed should be, distinguished from those substances constituting FUELS. In subsequently pursuing the significance of this distinction, we will again encounter the renewed applicability of George's profound perspicacity.

But for the present, let us continue on the path to capitalism in its early stages as suggested previously.

Stated baldly, of the three factors of production—labor, land, and capital—capital itself the amalgam of labor and land (defined as all natural endowments) has assumed an ascendancy impossible to have imagined prior to the Industrial Revolution. Simple tools and early machinery, multiplying the power of labor in employing "land," have metamorphosed into the most powerful and productive machines, within and without enclosing structures. The post-industrial era, up to and including the electronic and information revolutions, have only enhanced the overwhelming primacy of capital in relation to its companionate factors land and labor. This despite the indispensable application of labor to the functioning of capital in all its forms.

Although George clearly defined "land" as an economic factor encompassing all natural endowments, he has frequently used the term in the narrow sense of agricultural or commercial land. This is undoubtedly so because the earliest studies of relative land values and rent in Western Europe employed the term in its narrow sense. This was certainly true in the development of the Law of Rent. And the Law of Rent served George in logically establishing the persistent arrogation of a constantly increasing percentage of production to rent as development expands.

As was described earlier in this narrative, the Law of Rent is also applicable to agricultural, commercial, and in a particular but distinct manner, to industrial land as well. As was portrayed in the diagram in Chapter 16, indicating that in a geographically expanding economy, the return to labor in developed communities must exceed that of the return to labor in less developed communities, contrary to the dictates of the Law of Rent (otherwise known as the law of development). This is so because of the greater productivity of labor where an enhanced infrastructure and close proximity of productive forces makes higher wages mandatory and possible.

This perception also differs from George's acquiescence in the doctrine of prevailing uniform wage rates (mandated by the Law of Rent), and provides insight into one dynamic force propelling capital to its commanding position in greatly contributing to accelerating production.

Now, in its original sense, capital consisted of simple tools through which labor was applied to land. But with the geometric growth of technology, and increasing capital available for its development and implementation, capital now expressed in its monetary equivalent, was perceived as the prime force in generating production. It was this view which led to the theory of the "wages fund."

Capital in its monetary form, already defined as wealth devoted to the increase of wealth, shares certain attributes with land as a factor in economic production, and differs from it in certain unique ways.

Like land, it demands a return for its use in addition to the undiminished return of the asset made available for production.

Unlike land, capital is capable of undiminished growth, frequently requiring less and less "land" as part of the amalgam.

Both land and capital (in its monetary form making wages possible) are essential not only to modern production, but to human life itself (as wages or otherwise). It must be remembered that wages are defined as the return for human exertion, and are as economically applicable to those engaged in management, trade, all manner of services, as well as production.

We are now embarked upon an inquiry into the dynamics accounting for the enormous growth of capital in both absolute terms and as but one of the three factors of production.

Earlier it was pointed out that the primacy of land was impeached by the development of mills and simple workshops which, employing more (or even less) labor on a small parcel of land (often agriculturally useless land) could produce far more wealth than a similar-sized parcel of agriculturally productive land.

The capital and political power required thusly to challenge the landed aristocracy could only have come from those entrepreneurs constituting a mercantile (or trading) class. Their initial capital investments in shipbuilding and sea voyaging could only have come from an enlightened and venturesome element of the landed aristocracy itself. There could be no other source of venture capital other than the aristocratic "surplus."

The earlier economic order, advancing from the self-contained feudal estate to a semblance of village life, with tradesmen constituting a petty bourgeoisie, in time gained a semblance of political autonomy. With a gradual diminution of economic and religious constraint, economic and political initiatives slowly expanded. The slow but persistent growth of the petty bourgeoisie in wealth and in consequent political latitude assumed a spiraling effect which has continued through the centuries with the capitalist heirs of the petty bourgeoisie virtually commanding the political order of capitalist society today.

The establishment of corporate economic entities on the basis of shares, chartered and encouraged in every way by the political establishment in its thrall, made possible the arrogation of far flung assets to corporate coffers—with the elimination of personal accountability on the part of corporate organizers.

In the normal course of events, land as an economic factor of production, was itself incorporated, with shares bought and sold on the various exchanges. In just such manner has land, as a factor of production, been subsumed by capital.

29

THE DOMINANCE OF CAPITAL

The dominance of capital vis a vis the other two factors of production, land and labor, has been irrefutable for at least the entire twentieth century, and continues to this day. This is certainly true in the industrialized nations of the world.

The continued dominance of land as the most consequential factor of production continues only in those backward or tribal lands still ruled by a landed aristocracy. Much of the conflict between the industrialized (capitalist) nations and the undeveloped or developing nations still maintaining a feudal land structure stems from the inherent dynamic of pressure by the capitalist economies upon non-capitalist economies.

In a prior chapter a conceptual example was portrayed of the incipient emergence, or flowering, of a capitalist enterprise from a feudal base only recently tolerating the emergent bourgeoisie. While multitudes of books exist which describe the rise of capitalism and the mechanisms of the "free market," its vicissitudes, the effects of full and partial monopolies, restriction on international trade and its consequences, the emergence of a proletariat to provide labor for the expanding industrial system, etc., etc., there exists little discussion of the nature or the dynamics of an economic system at such variance with the static land-centered economies which had preceded it.

An early attempt at explaining the dynamics of an economic system in which consumption played a concurrent role to that of production was the promulgation of Say's law. Say's law, succinctly phrased, is that production generates consumption. Stated without explanation, it will almost certainly require explication, as the apparent equivalency means nothing. Nor is there the slightest intimation of a dynamic factor at work.

From the law's statement above, one would be justified in writing the equation P=C, or plotted on a two dimensional grid, would describe the following:

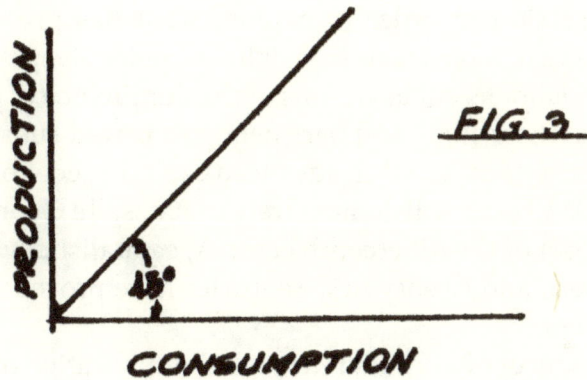

FIG. 3

a straight line bisecting the abscissa and ordinate bases. No dynamic is evident here.

One might also display said law graphically as:

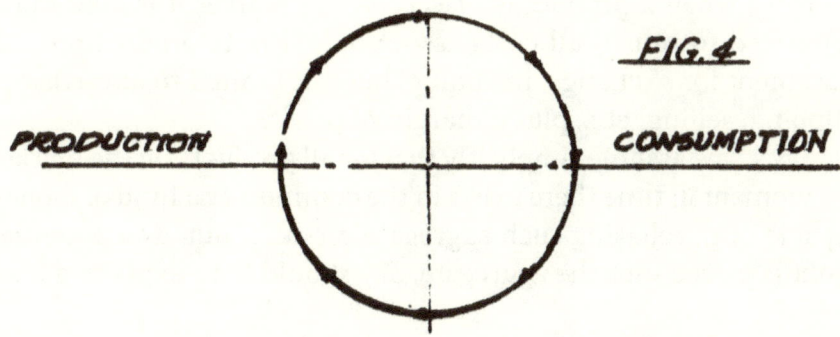

FIG. 4

Representation as a circularity also fails to illuminate the implied cause and effect relationship which a dynamic system mandates.

What Say's Law, in fact, wishes to express is that the expenditures of money for the use of land, labor, and capital engaged in production provide the purchasing power within the community for the consumption of that which is produced.

Now, that concept, crude as it is, lays the groundwork for an understanding of capitalist—as compared to pre-capitalist economic understanding. While true, it is simplistic and fails in various ways to describe much that is observable in the operation and expansion (or contraction) of a capitalist economy.

The reader is here reminded that this narrative has proceeded in this direction in order to explore what has previously been described as a demonstrable oversight by Henry George in equating capital and labor as equal victims of the dominance of private land ownership. The unique and pertinent role played subsequently by certain elements of "land" in advanced capitalist economies will be dealt with later, and will demonstrate that despite George's error in the latter part of the nineteenth century, capitalist development in the twentieth and twenty-first centuries have proved him correct and prescient.

The producer of a product through the application of labor upon "land," whether or not employing capital in the form of tools or machinery, if the product is marketable, is in fact creating wealth. If the product itself is utilizable in producing greater wealth (with the application of "land" and labor), that product is deemed capital, or wealth utilized in creating greater wealth.

Now, when a product is placed on the market it is (and must be) priced to return all costs associated with its production and placement for exchange, including, but not limited to advertising, shipping, selling, etc., plus a margin of profit.

Say's Law assumes implicitly that for all products on the market at a moment in time there exists in the community a fund of money capable of purchasing such aggregate product. But, as a potential profit is priced into the aggregate, Say should have explained how and from what source such added purchasing power was to come into play.

This incremental quantity cannot come from consumer savings, as that withholding would have failed to complete a prior cycle. One is obliged to conclude that only the profits from a prior cycle (or borrowings on it) expended primarily in the purchase of capital equipment, could possibly complete the cycle under consideration.

Barring these profits as inconsequential at the earliest stages of capitalist production, credit extended (by landowners and mercantilists) for capital investment would now serve as the required incremental consumption.

The enlarging spiral of production (and consumption) can now be seen as representing the dynamic introduced by invested profit and/or credit.

The process may be represented as indicated below;

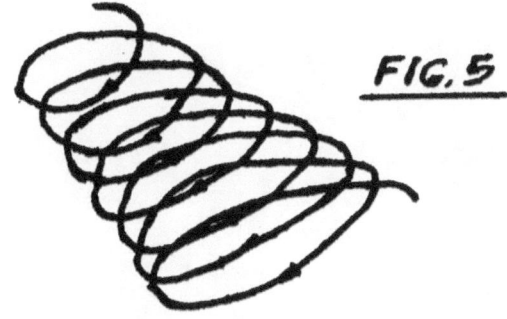

FIG. 5

where the constantly increasing radius of the spiral represents the magnitude of production/consumption per annum (the spacing of spirals remaining constant at a year).

Investment and/or credit are, of course, voluntarily provided in a sanguine economic climate. When a vigorous economic expansion weakens and prospects for a safe and high rate of return to capital begin to diminish, capital in the form of prior profits and/or credit may be withheld, and production/consumption will recede along the curvature of the spiral portrayed.

Say implicitly (and wrongly) assumed that capital in the form of prior profits and/or credit would always be available to complete the production/consumption equivalency, which would also preclude the business cycle phenomenon. While shedding light on the role of consumption in supporting production in a capitalist economy, Say failed to understand the economy's inherent dynamism, either positively in expansion or negatively in contraction.

30

CAPITALISM'S DYNAMISM

The implications of capitalism's inherent dynamism are vast, setting in motion events which are often unpredictable and/or uncontrollable.

Needless to say, purists and compromised economists will insist upon a mathematical representation of the premises set forth in the train of Say's theory. One is reminded of John Maynard Keynes' attempt, during the depths of the Great Depression, to portray to President Franklin Roosevelt a mathematical proof that, while a free economy will eventually return to equilibrium, that equilibrium may be at an intolerably low level of production and consumption. Keynes therefore recommended that purchasing power be placed in the hands of consumers by any means necessary, including governmental deficit financing. Roosevelt had instinctively anticipated his learned guest's remedy by previously having had enacted various job creating programs for public works improvements.

Henry George had addressed the phenomenon of business cycles in terms of speculation in land, but the phenomenon of sharpening competition during robust economic expansion by manufacturers, leading to excessive production in relation to demand, contributed to contraction of business activity as well as deflated land values. Expansive industrial activity invariable brings into play more producers and increasing costs of borrowing, thereby causing the most vulnerable producers to be the first to falter as business activity subsidies.

George described the profits of an enterprise as essentially a return on capital after rewarding land and labor with their share of the yield of production. It is this return on capital (frequently retained in the corporation's coffers for reinvestment) which promotes, through similar actions of all enterprises, the enlargement of the current spiral's radius. Credit—borrowing at a prevailing interest rate—with a view to earnings in excess of that rate facilitating repayment, provides identical promotion as described above. The greatest corporate entities carry extraordinarily large burdens of debt, as does the Federal Government—in an effort to promote growth. Frequently, government borrowing to enhance consumption operates contrapuntally to corporate expansion, as when production recedes along the current spiral.

Recessions, characterized by diminishing investment and consumption (frequently in reverse order), do not automatically occur. Where the economic outlook is perceived as unfavorable, corporate capital is withheld, and for a time is invested, not in plant and machinery, but in financial instruments yielding the generally prevailing rate of interest. The "generally prevailing rate of interest" is a term long debated in concept, as has been the justification for interest itself.

The argument is frequently advanced by those representing the interests of corporations and the wealthy, particularly during a recessionary period, that a cut in tax rates for these sectors would provide additional resources for investment by corporations in plant and machinery, and by the rich in all manner of enterprises.

Experience supports no such argument, nor does logic. The mere possession of additional assets in the coffers of a corporation will not induce investment by management in greater or more modern capacity in the face of a continuing cloudy economy. As for wealthy individuals, additional sums are likely to be spent in bidding up the price of non-productive assets or in the purchase of stocks at reduced prices in speculation on future price increases. Sums so spent provide no additional funds to the corporation, nor if they did, would they be spent on expansion as described above.

Henry George was of the opinion that interest, being natural, is desirable. He referred to the natural increase of animal stocks with only slight input of labor, and described the "prevailing rate of interest" as reflecting that natural increase.

Counter arguments can be presented both in logic and experience, however. For example, the natural increase in animal stocks cannot proceed indefinitely, but only so far as the fences of neighboring farms or ranches make possible. Yet interest, although fluctuating inversely with the stock of capital, continues under virtually all times and conditions.

While even in the Great Depression interest was paid for the loan of capital, at a very low rate to be sure, in recent years an interest rate of zero in Japan during a long recession failed to induce borrowing for stimulus of the economy. If interest is indeed a phenomenon based upon natural growth, surely a generally prevailing rate of zero should not have been reached.

31

THE MECHANICS OF THE CAPITALIST CORNUCOPIA

The extraordinary potency of profits generated in the spiraling market place has led in the past two and a quarter centuries of industrial production to a cornucopia of such wealth as the world has never previously experienced. The phenomenon has also generated much serious criticism that the "surplus value" so effective in this generative process represents unremitting theft of labor.

But so many revolutionary social, political, economic, and environmental changes have followed in the train of this self-perpetuating capitalistic mechanism, that singling out the issue of the justice of appropriating "surplus value" as the primary negative consequence appears off the mark. Even socialistic economies have felt obliged to imitate this capitalist mechanism to promote development.

Hopefully, it is understood by the reader that treating the factors of production as phenomena independent of human agency is simply a means of studying them apart from the human elements which animate those who play one or more of the three roles available to them. Fiction is, and has been, the appropriate and effective vehicle for dealing with land owner, laborer, or capitalist. As noted by Thorstein Veblen, there is very limited latitude for the capitalist to exercise independent, counter-class behavior without putting his own enterprise, as well as his political and social connections, in peril. This is, and always was true for the individual landowner, though somewhat universally true for the laborer, who is, from the economic point of view, defined as one whose share of production is granted in return for human exertion at any level.

Along the road from petty bourgeoisie to capitalist there arose the concept of "natural rights," in which it was generally accepted that a man (and it was invariably applicable to men) rightly owned that product into which he had integrated his solitary labor. This progressive notion had undoubtedly arisen to guaranty to the craftsman and tradesman rights which were non-existent under feudalism or, further back in history, under actual slavery.

The full development of capitalist production, where the product or products produced incorporated the limited labor input of many working men gradually nullified the working man's "natural right to any such product. In its place arose in legislation the right to contracted wages as a force in law.

It was, of course, essential to maintaining labor's capacity to consume as well as produce, in furtherance of the spiral of production/consumption, which made possible the early passage of elemental laws guarantying pay for work performed.

The dynamism of capitalist industrial production, generating greater and greater sums of capital demanding opportunities for investment, propelled not only local and national development, but gradually altered the mercantile system of cheap purchase abroad and expensive sale at home. The new imperial enterprise was one of seizing locations abroad suitable for, at first, agricultural exploitation, then eventually for industrial exploitation of an indigenous labor force.

Imperialism is, of course, much older than capitalism, with roots in antiquity, where absolute extinction or enslavement was the fate of the losing side of imperial aggression. A surplus was essential to the side mobilizing for seizure of adjacent lands and the eventual enslavement of the defeated, as well as for the defenders of such onslaught, but no existing economic mechanism mandated aggression in order to avert economic regression and stagnation.

It was only with the full development of industrial capitalism, establishing the symbiosis of essential, stimulated consumption acting as a form of flywheel to industrial production that global imperialism by Western industrial powers came into full development.

Whereas human greed and power lust were the engines of production for imperial export to subjugated lands and people reduced to selling raw materials to be worked up in the imperial homeland and shipped back as manufactured products to the captive colony for sale, the fuel for such enterprises was the hazard imposed in the imperial homeland of capital investment stagnation. Recessions, otherwise known as market collapses or economic crises, were experienced, though not well understood, very early in the capitalist era.

That is not to say that cyclical (actually, spiraling) capitalism is the economic equivalent of a railroad locomotive accelerating out of control, but means of guaranteeing that the locomotive remain on the tracks, while much improved, have by no means been developed or implemented.

32

CAPITALISM'S INHERENT MOMENTUM

It was earlier stated (Chapter 30) that the consequences of capitalism's inherent dynamism are vast, in fact, so vast that they have set in motion forces and events which effect every aspect of our lives—economic, political, social, and cultural. These consequences flow directly from the fact that the dynamic system previously described has forced all inherited and evolved institutions to assume a form conducive to the full play of the consumption/production spiral.

Clearly, if the stability of the system requires the fullest possible consumption of all production in a cycle, then inducing a turnover rate of said production in half a cycle will produce virtually twice the return. This simple fact will explain the ever-increasing pace of consumption induced by the advertising industry and all media encompassed by it—newspapers, magazines, television, the internet, telemarketing, etc.

On the production side, such increased pace of capital return (and profits, as George stated, were essentially a return on capital) would find its way to increased investment in new technologies, via research and development, whereby new consumer and producer products would further propel the consumption/production spiral outward.

The point being made here is that these accelerating, spiraling movements within the capitalist system, despite the real and apparent agencies of human greed, inventiveness, curiosity, power lust, etc. are mechanically inherent and merely provide fulfilling opportunities for the previously described human traits.

No other creature on earth could possibly invent such a dynamic economic system, since no other is capable of managed production for the purpose of impersonal consumption via exchange.

In the train of capitalist production/consumption, constantly consummated through exchange, the entire culture is altered to accommodate the means and methods of production, with consequent changes in inherited political and social arrangements within the culture.

As but one example, prior to industrialization, a uniquely capitalist development, there existed no proletarian (working) class to speak of.

A primitive form of cottage industry had developed to permit essentially agrarian workers, utilizing necessarily idle time, to fabricate certain simple products—first and foremost cloth.

The evolution of a class of artisans and tradesmen, as previously mentioned, from complete dominance by the landed class, to a bourgeoisie capable of suborning and then dominating their prior aristocratic masters, peacefully and through revolution when necessary, to today's democratic state, is just another example of economic and political changes resulting from the consumption/production dynamic.

Clearly, momentous economic, social, and political changes will produce significant and irreversible cultural changes as the consumption/production spiral advances, as well as when it reverses to a reduced consumption/production radius.

What has been laid out in this chapter are the broad strokes of capitalism's dynamism - generally expansive, and frequently reversible. The unique nature of capitalist dynamism may be best elucidated by comparing it with the economic system operative in the former Soviet Union, an ostensibly socialist model.

In accordance with Say's Law, production should be absorbed as consumption through the expenditure of the costs of said production. Since profit was not normally added to production costs, in accordance with Marxist doctrine, perfect circularity should have been achieved, similar to that prevailing in primitive societies. Such circularity would have ensured economic stagnation, whereas rapid economic expansion under a planned economy was the goal.

A different form of dynamism was achieved by the state's practice of distributing to labor a relatively minor portion of the value of production, in the form of a claim on consumer goods, while appropriating the larger part of production for capital investment and military needs.

These capital goods, once on line and generally reproducing themselves, permitted a very rapid growth in productive capacity, with a marginally increasing portion dedicated to the production of consumer goods.

Simply stated, rapid industrialization was achieved by the continual expropriation by the state of the largest part of wealth created by labor and capital.

No inherent dynamism resided in the presumptive socialist doctrine or performance. A dynamic rate of development devoid of transactional exchange was promoted and enforced by the state through central planning and coercion.

The social and political environment in which such "socialist" production/consumption might be maintained could only be authoritarian, with dissenting voices or behavior criminalized and punished as such, and propaganda (advertising) ensuring social acceptance of ceaseless poverty amidst increasing industrial wealth.

In pursuing its object of first containing and eventually causing the implosion of the Soviet Union, the United States took a page from the Soviet's economic book. Enormous sums were allocated to America's military and arms industries, thereby forcing the Soviets to increase the percentage of their overall production for military purposes, in order to maintain some sort of parity with the U.S.A., to a point where the remaining production for civil uses was so reduced as to render their society dysfunctional. The U.S. economy suffered in this pursuit only to the extent that poorer elements were further impoverished and social tensions between "haves" and "have nots" were heightened.

The following chapters will flesh out in greater detail the present human economic, social, political, and cultural conditions deriving from the inherent dynamism prevailing in the capitalist world—and which is constantly spreading globally.

The reader will have noted that no value judgments have heretofore been expressed in describing the capitalist phenomenon.

33

CAPITALISM REQUIRES INNOVATION

If the average American old enough to have experienced the great changes of the latter half of the twentieth century were asked to what he or she would attribute such changes, the answer would likely be the enormous technological advances in all fields.

Such answer would be superficially correct, but fundamentally in error.

Following upon the earlier description of the spiraling incremental growth of the consumption/production dynamism of a capitalist economy, technological development must be seen, not as a basic cause, but as the secondary effect in accommodating the necessary investment function propelling the accelerating spiral. New products, incrementally beneficial or revolutionary in improving the human condition, are absolutely essential in absorbing the wages and capital expended in their production.

Cyclical stability is not only intolerable, but virtually impossible; and where it momentarily exists is but a signal that the consumption/production cycle has transitioned to reverse. It is this point of the spiral which denotes the beginning of a recession, only much later recorded as two consecutive quarters with negative growth.

On the consumption side, in the second half of the twentieth century, can be seen the explosive growth of products and services which are not merely incidental to the proliferation of new technologies, but in fact play frivolously into the essential need for ever-increasing consumption to maintain the dynamism of the expanding consumption/production spiral.

The newly enhanced avenues of consumption are frequently of such a nature as to be explicable not solely in terms of entrepreneurial profits, but are performing a much more essential role in buoying the economy.

Surely, it is not accidental that the designation "throw-away economy" has arisen in the full development of a culture of consumption.

For centuries, if not millennia, human beings have lived in cultures of scarcity, but that economic environment began to change with the development of capitalism.

The variety of simple economic activities preceding the full flowering of late twentieth century capitalism has grown enormously in response to capital's insatiable need to thrust the production/consumption cycle further out in pursuit of dynamic stability for the system.

Musicians, singers, actors, athletes, and entertainers of all manner, at one time largely itinerant and generally eking out a hand to mouth existence, while generally experiencing social scorn, today are part and parcel of an enormous entertainment industry via motion pictures, radio, television, the internet, etc. In every case, venture capital is not only available, but presses funds into innovative entrepreneurial ventures.

Extraordinary medical innovations in surgical technology, pharmacology of greater potency and specificity, and hospitals with specialized treatment facilities have proliferated to the point where the health care industry now approximates fourteen percent of our gross domestic product.

Travel, both domestic and foreign, once a privileged activity of the wealthy, has grown to enormous proportions, with tourist revenues by many cities and countries now a large component of their annual incomes.

The automobile industry, basically subsidized by governmental financing of a vast road system, is an essential component of overall production investment propelling the production/consumption spiral.

Housing and construction, also promoted by prodigious government efforts to maintain low interest rates, also serve as a means for capital investments adding to the gross national product, synonymous with orbiting along the production/consumption spiral.

Many of the industries mentioned have a symbiotic relationship with each other, for example: travel with hotel construction and operation and the aircraft building industry; medical advances with hospital and treatment facility construction and operation; the automobile and home furnishings, etc., etc.

That the quality of life for many has been greatly enhanced (and extended) through the phenomena elucidated, is undeniable, but the lives of many remain unimproved materially, while suffering acutely from the negative effects of accelerating economic activity.

It is noteworthy that mature industries such as railroads, shipbuilding, steel making, the cloth and clothing industries, etc., having played out their roles in propelling their production/consumption functions, presently languish and receive virtually no serious governmental subsidies.

For those who find it difficult, if not impossible, to accept the first cause principle advanced in this narration, the present condition of the food industry, agriculture being our largest, the following argument is advanced.

The U.S. government has for some time now been charting the increase in obesity among our citizens, particularly our children.

The method by which the food industry, particularly the fast food industry, increases the volume of its sales, namely its income, is through techniques such as intensive advertising, deliberately over-sized portions laced with taste-enhancing fat, gifts, games, and factory-like production and service.

Can it be reasonably argued that technological innovation is the prime mover in the progressive growth of this industry nationally—and internationally? No, it is the unrelenting pressure of capital requiring ever expanding opportunities for the enhanced investment returns of aggregating capital to propel the production/consumption spiral further out.

Conventional economic discourse persists in advocating policies promoting expansion. The federal government is ever vigilant in assessing the hazards of recession, and implements fiscal policies to ensure expansion, while the Federal Reserve Bank functions monetarily, nominally independently, to promote the same outcome.

In light of the above, is it still possible to doubt the first principle thesis of capitalism's inherent expansionary trajectory along an expanding production/consumption spiral?

34

INHERITED CULTURE AND CAPITALISM

Of the numerous ramifications of capital's dynamism, the most significant for the social critic and historian will surely continue to be its impact upon contemporary culture. The signs and symptoms of both burgeoning and declining societies and civilizations have always manifested themselves in cultural terms, if one only looked beneath the surface of mundane, non-dramatic occurrences.

Contemporary western culture, presently spread through most of the worlds capitalist (and approaching-capitalist) economies may be described as the third derivative of capitalist production/ consumption dynamism, following that of the technological expansion.

If one looks closely at most aspects of contemporary culture, its capitalist genesis is readily visible, i.e.: popular entertainments, at one time only marginal to western society, from the Athenian theatre to medieval England onto Shakespeare and the Elizabethans, has swelled to a considerable segment of the nation's economy, by a deliberate pandering, in intellectual and moral content, to the lowest common denominator. This "dumbing down," no longer even touted as a form of democratization, is simply a means to extend the market as fully down the base of the educational pyramid as possible. The cultural consequences, however, are to reduce standards of thought and expression to that of the "mob," so dreaded and despised by even would-be democratically-minded elites of the past.

This "mob," having so vastly enriched media moguls while the "mob's" tastes and morals have been promoted as the newest prevailing standards, can become convinced of its "democratic" power, and must therefore be wooed as an electorate.

Inherited, historically respected art forms, such as sculpture, painting musical composition, drama and literary fare have become the almost exclusive possessions of a shrinking elite, with forms of expression in the arts in contemporary culture having adopted the market place characteristics of novelty, provocation, sentimentality, mindlessness, amorality and vulgarity.

Sexual freedom and candor, salutary in itself, has not only fueled a licit and illicit industry, but has for market place gain, debased the values of responsibility, constancy, loyalty and the realistic need to work toward conjugal harmony and stability. Instant gratification—as infantile desire—is promoted in the service of consumer product turnover, ultimately rendering human beings themselves disposable.

The move from a "Coca Cola" culture to a "Kleenex" culture certainly stems from capitalism's production/consumption dynamism; but the cultural consequences are fraught with danger.

The educational system, a contemporary growth industry, in addition to participating in propelling the production/consumption spiral forward (the product being the student), examined as a cultural asset, is seen to be defective in its production at the lowest to medium levels, self serving of its managing elite, and at its highest levels suborned and subservient to its financial supporters from government to corporate contributors.

Universities, one of the first incorporated entities, having achieved unimagined freedom under feudal dominion, have settled into the comfortable knowledge business, having promoted its product as indispensable in a consumer economy.

Government itself, at all levels, while stressing its democratic lineage to ancient Athens (a slave state), actively promotes the ethos of "natural rights" in an advanced capitalist economy which renders such humanist concept irrelevant.

The bondage of representative government to the owners and managers of corporations large and small, with their armies of shameless "lobbyists," has alienated citizen voters from the political process in droves and driven them to the trivial pursuits of ceaseless entertainment, diversion and locust-like consumption.

The social and cultural consequences of this grand alienation from community participation and involvement tends to atomize the citizenry and erode the inherited culture, without significant incremental addition.

The corporate structure, the dominant means of propelling capitalist dynamism along the production/consumption spiral, itself an inherently undemocratic entity, has corrupted and undermined the democratic political structure devised by the founding fathers of the republic. So corrupt has the corporate structure become, absent political control, that many corporations have been exposed as run by and for corporate leaders who have turned their firms into criminal enterprises. The most prestigious investment banking houses and brokerage firms, in an almost universal falling away of standards of integrity and probity, have been implicated in a cascading breakdown of inherited cultural values.

The preceding litany of economic, social, and cultural imperatives clearly are offspring of the capitalist dynamic phenomenon.

More will be written later as to the likely future of the capitalist system.

35

FUEL AS A NATURAL ENDOWMENT

The thesis set forth heretofore is that a capitalist economy is propelled by the differential between market value and production costs exacted through exchange. Profit is that differential, and distinguishes a capitalist transaction from sheer barter in a primitive pre-capitalist, pre-money economy.

The seemingly reasonable insistence upon a return of profit, above and beyond one's costs of production, when obtainable in the market place, is the element which provides for capitalist dynamism along an accelerating spiral. It is this dynamism which is responsible for the good and evil flowing from capitalist production and consumption.

It is fairly obvious that such a production/consumption spiral is capable, with each completed round, of creating increased capital value of geometric scale. When in reverse, the loss is of similar magnitude.

The thesis advanced by Henry George, and predicated upon Ricardo's Law of Rent, established the basis for the conclusion that as land of lesser productivity, which can be exploited rent free, is brought into production, the rightful value of rent in the more productive lands of the community is that portion of overall production on such land in excess of the productivity of rent free land. The relationship is more readily demonstrated graphically.

The point stressed here is the clearly implied, if understated, dynamism of the mechanism.

Consequently, pre-capitalist development (as per Ricardo's Law of Rent) and capitalist development, in its entirety, are characterized by the pivotal roles of incremental growth and reinvestment of those increments. This should not be surprising, as organic growth from the former to the latter is readily apparent.

As regards the geometric growth of capital in advanced capitalist societies, one has only to observe the vast wealth in the coffers of banks and insurance companies, entirely disengaged from material participation in the production/consumption spiral. Inasmuch as investment banks actively promote the sale of shares of corporations to institutions and the general public (retaining as fee for service substantial shares), and organize the sale of bonds of corporations, or purchase of same, the application of the fruits of "surplus" production of the production/consumption cycle falls principally on these institutions.

That such accumulation of "excess" capital exists and forcefully seeks investment in promising nations and regions has been apparent in recent years in the infusion and subsequent flight of capital from the far eastern "Little Tigers," Mexico, Argentina, etc.

Since wealth and capital (readily interchangeable) in monetary form represent a standing claim on land and labor, of which it was originally composed, a sustained lapse in its reintroduction into the production/consumption cycle can only precipitate unemployment and shrinkage of land values. Therefore, the welfare of the entire nation has come to depend upon the smooth working of the financial institutions entrusted with this function and explains the essentially subservient function of government in aiding in every possible way the retention of the dynamic stability of the production/consumption spiral.

An extremely important factor, almost entirely overlooked in studies of the transition from a land-based, essentially agricultural economy into a capitalist economy is the role of that species of land (or natural endowment) constituting fuels. Capitalist production without mechanical tools and machinery would scarcely be capitalism at all; and the machinery of production without fuels, or energy derived from fuels, would be impossible. It is this essential fact which turns our inquiry back to the issue of the role of land as a factor of production.

It is, in fact, quite ironic that land (in the form of fuels) enabling capital (in the form of machinery) should have reversed the undeniable former dominance of capital as among the three factors of production.

There can be little doubt that the corporations, generally international, which control the production of oil, gas, coal, and fissionable material have pre-empted the primacy of the great manufacturing industries. Automobile and truck production and usage, steel and aluminum production and usage, air, sea, and ground transportation, etc., would all grind to a halt without supplies of largely fossil fuels. The monetary equivalents of fuel as "land" and machinery of production as capital display the same reversed hierarchy.

World-wide steel production is shrinking as plastic production (petroleum based) grows. Revenues of capital intensive industries continue to shrink, while the revenues of fuel manufacturers, also capital intensive, continue to grow. It is almost as if the latest phase of capitalized production has come to resemble the world of land dominance as studied and written about by Henry George in Progress and Poverty.

All of which raises the question posed and eventually answered by George: why the increase of poverty with progress—or greater overall material wealth? George showed that this was due to labor and capital (?) receiving a smaller and smaller share with a lowering "margin of production," the largest percentage going for rent to landowners. Now, can this analysis possibly be applicable to the era following the latter third of the twentieth century as "land" (in the form of the sources of fuel) began to displace the regime of capital (in the form of machinery)? Has not an ever increasing share of overall wealth in the U.S.A. been passing into the hands of a smaller and smaller segment of the population?

If the results are so similar, isn't it possible that the mechanisms are essentially the same. Let us explore that possibility.

In order to investigate the possibility (articulated above) that "land" as energy-supplying fuel sources, behaves very much as did land as agricultural natural endowment, let us imagine ourselves back in the English midlands in the early eighteenth century.

On the lands owned by several aristocrats, which provided these landowners with rent from tenant farmers, mines have been sunk by other tenants engaged in extracting coal. The reason why we speak of tenancy of land in terms of wealth production is that aristocratic owners would never farm their own lands—not to speak of engaging in coal extraction.

The mines are not equally productive, in consequence of differing depths of coal seams, capital investment, management, and available labor. Rent, presumably consisted of payment per ton and would likely be adjustable in accordance with the terms of a long-term lease. Consequently, overall payment of rent would differ from estate to estate.

Such situation would be analogous to the assumption of Ricardo's Law of Rent as regards agricultural production.

Let us consider, in our imaginings, that an aristocratic landowner in the vicinity, possessing a patch of infertile or otherwise unexploitable land, harbors the hope that coal may be found under such land. To induce a coal mining company to invest in exploiting the possibility of finding coal, he offers rent free exploitation of coal findings for a number of years, with proscribed excessive exploitation of coal during the period.

Assuming that such scheme is successfully completed, and coal is found and exploited as agreed upon, we now have an almost perfect analogy of Ricardo's Law of Rent, where the margin of cultivation is established where "land" free of rent established the justifiable payment of rent by other "lands" in terms of the productivity of "land" exploited rent free.

In accordance with the Law of Rent, the true claim by the landlord of rent is the portion of return above the horizontal productivity line where rent is zero, just as is the case with agricultural activity.

The difference between coal and agricultural production is that coal is a wholly depletable product, and agricultural production is only slightly so, never-the-less requiring some annual restitution. This distinction will be discussed later.

As the return to capital and labor in the more productive mining operations is no more than is the case of the no-rent mining operation, the percentage of overall production taken as rent, just as in the case of agriculture, is much greater than where rent is zero—or to any extent, at least within a reasonable range.

Aside from the question of depletion, coal, as a mineral extracted from land, can be seen to follow the same Law of Rent established by Ricardo for agricultural land, The implication of this similarity, in light of the present primacy of fuels as against manufacturing capital is very significant.

Needless to day, the extraction of other fuels or minerals in the same imagined circumstances, would lead to the same uneven distribution of production.

There is no apparent reason why the Law of Rent should not be operational in reverse, as described below.

On the international scene, where a long term petroleum production region, such as the Texas/Oklahoma fields have experienced declining production, and in comparison to it, newer producing areas such as undersea zones of the Gulf of Mexico, the north slope of Alaska, or the North Sea fields, can be regarded as "lands" of higher productivity, the Texas/Oklahoma fields may be considered as the lowest producer, rent free or not, by which the appropriate "rent" to higher producing "lands" may be determined.

While the international market price of petroleum is determined by many factors, such as the grade or "sweetness" of the oil itself, the relative transportation costs to a particular customer or region, in terms of legitimate "rent" per barrel per acre of oil field, the "rent" per barrel, per acre of the lowest producer is the determinant.

The application of the Law of Rent to international fuel (as "land" or natural endowment) is necessarily complicated by the issues of surface land ownership versus sub-surface mineral rights, varying quality of the product, and moreover by the cartelization of much of the industry by giant international oil companies for whom presumptively sovereign states act in masking roles, in activities which, within a law-abiding state, would constitute collusion in restrain of trade, and consequently illegal.

It is not necessary to vigorously apply the Law of Rent to the operations of the international oil, gas, coal, or uranium trade in order to affirm the dominance of fuel (as land) over industrial plant (as capital) in a reversal of the dominance of the latter between the onset of the eighteenth century and the middle of the twentieth. Nowhere is industry so cartelized (and therefore exercising monopoly power) as in the international fuel industry.

It can hardly be doubted that, although both the manufacturing industry and the energy industry are traded on the stock and bond markets of the globe, it is the fuel industry which is truly more dominant.

36

SURPLUS VALUE

The thesis advanced here is that Capitalism is best understood as a dynamic economic system perpetually accelerated by the reinvestment of "surplus value" in the economy in the form of capital. When reinvestment is withheld, the system decelerates in the same manner. The system is best portrayed as a spiral with a constantly increasing radius over time (indicating day to day growth) and spiral elements spaced arbitrarily at a year.

Inevitably, even a constant infusion of capital investment into the system would induce exponential growth with all its benefits and hazards. This capital infusion may be postponed for brief periods of time, but cannot be held idle indefinitely without reverting to wealth; and in the competition between institutions like banks and insurance companies earning solely through the investment of capital, capital investment becomes virtually mandatory.

Unstated, even the relatively simple Law of Rent implies a degree of growth, if only in an enlarging population requiring expansion to less productive lands.

Inasmuch as it is in the nature of Capitalism, operating like a producer of compounding interest, to create constantly increasing wealth for reinvestment, it normally requires a growing labor input to turn "land" into wealth and therefore more capital.

Consequently, it can be argued that under modern Capitalism, enlargement of population is mandatory and economically beneficial, not only for productive labor input, but also for labor's role as consumer of the enlarged output of product. Increased profits are a consequence of this phenomenon.

This result can be observed in the swelling growth of productivity in lands which have encouraged immigration—lands such as the U.S.A., Canada, Australia, Argentina, and even Israel. Newly opened lands present an abundant source of "land," which an increasing supply of labor readily transforms into wealth, hence capital. "Land" in the form of natural endowment other than agricultural or commercial land, plays the same role and, as previously stated, presently has overtaken the market power of industrial production, with fuel resources considered the most predominant "land," or natural endowment.

Capitalism, where it has been allowed to develop freely, unencumbered by government control, debilitating corruption, or a work force indifferent to material improvement as balanced against the harsh regimen of the factory system, can, and has produced wealth virtually unimagined in prior eras.

However, negative conditions and circumstances persist which are endemic to this great productivity, including but not limited to great wars among advanced, competing capitalist nations, and enduring unemployment of a large minority of a capitalistic society. It is this persistence of poverty within a capitalist society of great wealth and productivity which was the subject of Henry George's great work, and is in large measure the subject of this narrative.

Despite the absence of self-limiting factors in the enlargement of capitalist production, as portrayed in an enlarging spiral, and excepting the hazards of periodic contraction of the near-circular elements of the spiral, there are external factors which must, and will, limit or destroy the "wild horse" nature of Capitalism.

It is in the nature of advancing and ramifying technology, while continually creating new consumer products and engaging labor to create new wealth, to produce capital equipment which producers of all kinds purchase and employ to *limit and reduce* labor input and costs.

It is worth considering the long term consequences of this trend. But before proceeding with such consideration, the nature of constantly growing and ramifying technology itself bears analysis.

It is here contended that, like population growth, technological development is not an independent variable in the capitalistic dynamic. Technological advancement is responsive to the capital withheld from production for application to research and development of products and processes!

Such technological achievements then impact upon overall production levels.

There can be little doubt that technology is invested in by capital in order to increase production without increasing labor input, or to maintain production with ever-diminishing employment of labor.

The ideal factory would best resemble the automated petroleum refinery, where a handful of staff can maintain the facility and serve to monitor the automated equipment. Such plants, virtually devoid of significant labor input, understandably, are extremely profitable and are emulated by all manufacturers.

Now, while an automated manufacturing plant can be made more profitable through the reduction of its labor force, the impact of such phenomenon on society as a whole is quite another matter. What is "good for General motors" may be good for America, but what is good for overall automated or automating production facilities is definitely not good for the long term stability of society at large.

Remembering Say's Law, which identified all expenditures of production in monetary terms as the source of said consumption, a constant reduction in the labor force due to accelerating productive efficiency must reduce the capacity of labor to consume such production. While it is necessary and desirable for increased profits to encourage population increase, advancing technology operates in the opposite direction by a proportional reduction in the required labor force to generate this production.

While it is reputed that approximately one third of all capital investment is consumption of productive equipment and facilities, such consumption is (as I have already indicated elsewhere) entirely voluntary and therefore unreliable. A failure or reduction of this element of "consumption" is the basis for a retreat along the spiral path, and in common parlance is called a recessionary period.

Governments, in order to brake a continuing retreat along the spiral of production, invariable spends large sums for arms or social services (or both) and enact stimulative tax cuts to encourage capital investment, even if industry is operating at eighty percent of capacity, and is prepared to engage in large public borrowing to finance such stimulation.

The stability of a recessionary state can be precarious, and may retreat into deflation along the referenced spiral, a possibility against which John Maynard Keynes warned, and therefore prescribed stimulation of consumption.

Generally, demand on the consumer and producer side over time responds to real and perceived needs and the spiral forges ahead again.

A tree can no more "grow to the sky" than can such an economic system grow (of necessity) without end. Aside from the global economic and environmental impact of accelerating growth through stimulus, the devised methods have, among other effects, that of a continuing shift of productive wealth from labor to capital, as capital's role in production constantly enlarges.

The demand of capital for the lion's share of the nation's wealth is revealed in statistics indicating a great and growing disparity between the wealth and incomes of the rich (who constantly grow in wealth and numbers) and all others whose incomes and wealth continue to shrink as their numbers also grow.

Of course, this is a prescription for social and political instability with all the dire consequences which flow from such a condition.

The inequity outlined above, which will be stoutly defended by social Darwinists , was undoubtedly the position of the elites of all prior civilizations which have failed for "lack of commonweal" despite repeated efforts at reform.

However, never before has civilization had to face the environmentally adverse conditions flowing from the prevailing accelerating economic system.

It is hardly necessary to point out that a geometric increase of production, nationally and internationally, demands the input of greater and greater amounts of natural resources, primarily energy-providing resources. Whereas many natural resources can be preserved, in part, by recycling, energy resources cannot be. In fact, industrial efforts to recycle resources generally require a significant energy input.

Increased production and consumption understandably generate increased waste. Even non-industrial centers generate increasing waste requiring great efforts at disposal in order to avert increased health risks. A great deal of the solid waste generated in urban centers is not directly attributable to population numbers, but to the increased per capita consumption necessary to absorb increased production.

Land fills (themselves created in antiquity for health reasons, mutual defense, and economic coordination for more efficient production) must increasingly be relocated further into the hinterland.

However, the hazards of air, river, and sea pollution are not so readily dealt with. In short, the physical environment is increasingly incapable of bearing the abuses imposed by the spiraling growth of industrial and agricultural production. And ultimately, in the clash between the physical environment and accelerated capitalist development, such production must, and will be restrained—by human choice, or otherwise.

So while current capitalist development creates the contemporaneous risks of economic backsliding, with all present economic and political instabilities and hardships, continued, uncontrolled growth, being unsustainable, promises the almost certain breakdown and deterioration of the capitalist economic system.

Globalization, a more efficient and novel form of imperialism, illustrates on the international scene, the irresistible forward acceleration of the phenomenon of mandatory capital investment propelling the spiral of production.

Labor forces abroad present an irresistible wedding partner to domestic capital demanding investment. Domestic opportunities generally pale by comparison; and the cheaply manufactured products from abroad may be imported with the complicity of the taxing authorities, and with phenomenal profits. The overall effect on domestic labor need hardly be imagined; the export of good, well paying domestic jobs is more transparent every day.

Once semi-colonized nations were the helpless victims of the phenomenon described above. In somewhat less than half a century, several have themselves become manufacturing economies exporting not only product, but capital itself. Japan is one of the earliest examples of this development.

There are those who would point out that, as automated production increases and industrial jobs are lost, the excess labor force is increasingly absorbed into the service industries. However, such jobs almost invariably pay less than the industrial jobs lost, and furthermore, change in the service industries generally flows out of automation and causes a reduction of the required labor force.

37

CONSUMERISM AND CAPITALISM

The consumerist aspect of capitalism stems directly from conformance with Say's Law, with the inevitable concurrent burgeoning of advertising and all other means of product promotion to assure adequate consumption. Which is to assert that consumerism is by no means an independent development, but of the essence of capitalism's growth to its present dominance in conformance with the prior representation of an expanding "spiral" of production/consumption.

The cornucopia of capitalist production has raised a multitude of societies from communities of scarcity to communities of abundance—no mean accomplishment. But, of course, there is a dark side to this development, explored in depth by Henry George in his book *"Progress and Poverty."*

The dark side of this remarkable feat is emphasized in this narration because it is the dark side of capitalism's triumph which will ultimately lead to capitalism's deterioration and ultimate failure.

Reference has already been made to the effect of advancing technology, in factory and office, and of the reduced ability of a diminished, engaged labor force to consume its output in compliance with Say's Law.

A reduced work week to counter this trend has been tried in several countries, but inevitably it reduces labor's income as its hours of work are reduced. Friction among various labor elements is virtually inevitable. And although these conflicts are resolvable under extreme pressure, such successful resolution is incapable of altering the implacable movement toward greater automatic production with diminished labor input.

Related to the phenomenon described above, and deriving from the plethora of manufactured goods, many of little lasting value, which contribute to an unavoidable spiraling of solid and liquid waste disposal, is the increasing ecological damage resulting from the absorption and discarding of products due to the implacable appetite encouraged and necessitated by capitalist dynamism.

Obviously, clearing the shelves four times a year is more profitable than doing so once. And opening the doors of emporia to customers twenty-four hours a day, instead of eight or ten hours, must certainly accelerate sales and increase income.

Essential to sustaining the accelerating production/consumption cycle is advertising and marketing in general. Consumerism would be quite impossible without them. While the influence of advertising and marketing is beneficial to promoting greater consumption, and consequently production, their impact upon inherited, traditional customs and values which have sustained the culture is not.

Of course, there are those who have no interest in and express no nostalgia for the "old way," especially where the "newer" ways prove more profitable.

However, there are certain characteristics of the "new ways" which impact on increased production and consumption and thereby place the ecosystem at greater and greater peril. They also influence human behavior, public and private, through the context of advertisements as well as the entertainment sandwiched between commercials on television.

The fact is that the production/consumption cycle requires an ever-increasing market reach, and forces the advertising of products and services to the lowest cultural level in order to tap into the largest segment of the market. It is only a question of time until the manners and mores of this overwhelming body of consumers metamorphoses into the prevailing standards.

But it is just this vast majority of citizens who are relied upon to soberly choose those who govern us and exercise an influence on government in crucial matters.

Since advertising is designed to be essentially distracting, diverting and deceiving, a citizenry attuned to such manipulation loses the critical capacity to judge.

Now, an informed citizenry being essential to maintaining a democratic and representative form of government, a citizenry deceived and befuddled in matters of consumption are not likely to recognize the theft or distortions of their inherited liberties, and will eventually form a dissatisfied and destabilizing population jeopardizing the best aspects of capitalism.

38

THE FUTURE OF CAPITALISM

The scenario for capitalism's self-destruction, heretofore set forth, is likely to occur over a considerable length of time, but inescapable symptoms of eventual disintegration are ever present and increasing in number and magnitude. What passes for vitality in contemporary culture, and is encouraged by more ubiquitous and insistent advertising, directed primarily at the young, induces not only greater consumption, but greater immaturity and unsustainable self-indulgence. Heightened selfishness, however, is not compatible with the maintenance of the mortar of social harmony and democratic unity in diversity. Where the disparity between rich and poor (with a shrinking middle class under increasing pressure) continues to grow (internationally as well as domestically), historical examples point to more intense class conflict.

The ancient Athenian democracy (marred by slavery) revolved about the three focal points of: the temple, market, and governmental center. The evolution of these institutions into western culture has of late witnessed the apparently irresistible permeation by the market place into every other institution—temple, government, higher and lower education, etc. Today the market place (capitalist production and distribution) dominates and sets its system of values upon every aspect and element of society.

As feudalism is the derivative of failed slave states, capitalism is the natural outgrowth of feudal society, and in its failing will give rise to an as yet unclear economic and social order. That is the hopeful expectation; but the process itself is likely to be difficult and even violent, as the latter half of the twentieth century and opening years of the twenty-first have demonstrated.

The emergence of China and India as world powers seeking modified forms of capitalist development, and the struggle of a reconstructed Russia, shorn of her former empire, to redevelop, are surely harbingers of forces acting to reshape the classical capitalist world order. The extent to which the United States accommodates these new ventures in capitalism will determine in large measure the ease or difficulty of the birth of a new and more humane capitalism-of-sorts.

The vast majority of readers have surely found it extremely difficult and painful to accept the notion that historical forces beyond any one nation's, or generation's control have irresistibly shaped the economic and social society in which we live, and that the capitalist economic system essentially operates autonomously and unjustly where the earth's natural endowments are privately or corporately owned; and that, like its predecessors, in its present form will inevitably fail and disintegrate.

Having undertaken this inquiry in an effort to validate (and modify where required) the seminal work of Henry George's *Progress and Poverty*, the author has, by the use of George's intellectual tools, extended that inquiry from a post-feudal era to and through the early years of the twenty-first century.

The author has found that the inequities of private and corporate "land" ownership, wherein a larger and larger percentage of growing productive wealth is arrogated to a minority of possessors, functions in precisely the same manner, and with the same inevitable disintegrative results, where the term "land" is translated to "natural endowments" under advanced capitalism.

While capitalism in its traditional form is not reformable to the ideals of either libertarian or socialistic visionary, inherent internal contradictions and the irresistible forces of the natural environment and its protectors, will eventually check its mindless metastasis and force its modification to something other than capitalism as we have known it.

THE END

www.ingramcontent.com/pod-product-compliance
Lightning Source LLC
Chambersburg PA
CBHW032019170526
45157CB00002B/766